"To take one step in the direction of Shangri-La is
to be liberated from mundane existence."

—Eighth-century Tibetan sage

ULTRA
SURVIVAL KIT

Justin Lichter

FALCON GUIDES

GUILFORD, CONNECTICUT
HELENA, MONTANA

AN IMPRINT OF GLOBE PEQUOT PRESS

To buy books in quantity for corporate use or incentives, call **(800) 962–0973** or e-mail **premiums@GlobePequot.com**.

FSC
www.fsc.org
MIX
Paper from
responsible sources
FSC® C005010

FALCONGUIDES®

Copyright © 2014 Morris Book Publishing, LLC
ALL RIGHTS RESERVED. No part of this book may be reproduced or transmitted in any form by any means, electronic or mechanical, including photocopying and recording, or by any information storage and retrieval system, except as may be expressly permitted in writing from the publisher. Requests for permission should be addressed to Globe Pequot Press, Attn: Rights and Permissions Department, PO Box 480, Guilford, CT 06437.

FalconGuides is an imprint of Globe Pequot Press.
Falcon, FalconGuides, and Outfit Your Mind are registered trademarks of Morris Book Publishing, LLC.

Interior photos by Justin Lichter unless otherwise credited.

Text design: Sheryl P. Kober
Layout: Sue Murray
Project editor: Julie Marsh

Library of Congress Cataloging-in-Publication Data is available on file.

ISBN 978-0-7627-9020-3

Printed in the United States of America

The author and Globe Pequot Press assume no liability for accidents happening to, or injuries sustained by, readers who engage in the activities described in this book.

CONTENTS

CONTENTS

INTRODUCTION

Welcome to the Ultralight Survival Kit!

Hiking and backpacking are activities with low barriers to entry. Anybody can participate in them. They are rewarding and amazing, but skills and know-how come with experience. The calm and serenity of being in nature can quickly change into fear. Countless times I have seen people turn around and head back to the trailhead when the situation changes or, worse yet, continue and get in over their heads. I have had to make the same choices numerous times. Knowing when and where to turn back are just as important as the skills to handle unforeseen circumstances. This book will explain the skills you will need if you decide to push on, while still carrying minimal equipment to handle any situation you might encounter. It will explain in an easy-to-read format what to look for, how to overcome most situations you could face in the backcountry, and how to handle things if they take a turn for the worst.

This entire book is filled with "on trail" tips and skills. Initially it covers some skills that will help make your time in the wilderness more comfortable. Comfort and enjoyment are key ingredients to a successful trip. From there we move on to those "Oh $&!#" moments and everything you'll need to be prepared and remain safe. Too many people are hesitant to pare down their equipment into the lightweight and ultralight realms simply because of that "what if" situation. This book explains how to overcome those "what ifs" using what you would typically carry in a standard ultralight kit.

My goal is to get people outside. We need to reconnect with wilderness and value the remote places that we have left. I want you to have fun and experience the backcountry safely so that you aren't too intimidated to head out. Hopefully this book will help you accomplish that. I have trimmed and cut back anything extra or unnecessary from this book, similarly to what I have done with my own backpacking kit. It is streamlined so you that can carry this book along with you and read it on the trail. Reference it if or, I should probably say, when you get into a hairy situation. These circumstances are inevitable but overcoming them can make a trip that much more rewarding—and make for a great story afterwards!

Enjoy.

"TRAUMA"

—*Justin Lichter aka Trauma*

P.S. Remember to pack it in, pack it out; tread lightly; take only pictures, and leave only footprints; and practice Leave No Trace outdoors ethics. Visit LNT.org for more info.

Plan, Pack, and Get Organized

I can't stress the importance of planning enough. I live by the mantra "Prior proper planning prevents piss-poor performance." You can never plan too much; good planning will prevent or at least prepare you for the conditions and situations you might encounter.

When you are planning, it is crucial to look at the weather forecast, including potential high and low temperatures, trail conditions, the gear and equipment you will need and that will work best for those conditions (especially if you are doing anything technical) and any other conditions that might be applicable, such as snowpack, river flows, and avalanche forecasts. Planning also entails thoroughly researching the maps and routes to assess realistic daily mileage goals and possible campsites, as well as potential resupply locations. This all ties into how much food you will need to carry and what gear you will need.

When you are planning, it is important to weigh the pros and cons of your equipment for the conditions you are likely to face. This will help you slim down what you need to pack and decide such things as how warm a sleeping bag you should bring and what shelter you should pack. To help you get organized for your trip, I have incorporated a Gear Checklist (GC) into the back of this book. This list helps ensure that I don't forget anything when I am rushing to head out the door. I have learned from previous episodes of futility, where I set out and hiked to camp, only to realize that I had forgotten my tent stakes, ground sheet, lighter, or some other essential item. The GC also helps you easily visualize and itemize the weight of each piece of gear in the constant effort to eliminate unnecessary items and reduce weight.

Yoni is hard at work planning our trip. Spreading out is typical for when I plan a hike, especially when I am not following a commonly used trail. I will use a road map to show me the backcountry areas and possible resupplies. Then I will scale down to Benchmark state series maps, followed by actually mapping it on the AllTrails software. I will print out the maps from the software (cutting the white borders off the pages) and sometimes cut up the Benchmark maps to carry with me.

Keep Your Pack Light
without Sacrificing Essentials

There are hardly any true essentials of backpacking. There is a big difference between what you need and what you want. There is also a big difference between what you need and what you think you need. Ultralight or lightweight backpacking is simplicity. It's streamlining what you have on your back and what you are carrying until you whittle down your equipment to just what you are using regularly. Any other item is not a necessity. It helps to think outside the box and find multiple purposes for essential items.

Obviously you'll need some sort of backpack, shelter, and sleeping system. When choosing your equipment, remember that an ounce here and an ounce there will add up quickly. Ounces add up to pounds, and pounds add up to . . . heavy!

Despite camping at over 5100 meters (16,700 feet), ultralight is possible. Here we are using a Cuben fiber shelter and a trekking pole for the main support. Also since my friend Pepper and I are hiking together, we are able to share the shelter and split the communal gear to save weight.

Beyond your backpack, shelter, and sleep system, any thing is possible. Some ultralighters choose not to cook meals, so they don't have to carry a stove, pot, and fuel. Your clothing system will vary depending on where you go and what time of year. I never bring a full change of clothes. I choose to bring along additional layers, which makes my layering system more versatile for less weight. If you go a few days without using something you are carrying, you need to think twice about why and if you really need that piece of equipment.

Common Multipurpose Uses

- Tent stakes for a pot stand

- Trekking poles for tarp or shelter supports

- Skis or ice axes as tent stakes

- Backpack as the lower half of a sleeping pad

My nighttime spread consists of a half-length sleeping pad (shoulders to hips), tarp, shelter, or stuff sack filled for my pillow, extra gear in my pack to elevate my legs and serve as the lower half of my sleeping pad, and ultralight ground sheet.

- Digital camera photos as backup maps for small sections where maps don't overlap or for routes through technical areas. Also, you can take photos of contact information you might need in town.

- Extra clothes or your shelter, if the weather is good, as your pillow

>>> TIP: Mail items to yourself if you are on a longer hike that requires resupply. Send such things as your camera battery charger, extra maps, clothes you might need, and vitamins so that you won't have to carry them the entire time.

Tips to stay warm on a chilly night without carrying a heavier sleeping bag:
- Wear socks to sleep. Your feet will be the first part of your body that gets cold. This quick and easy fix can help prevent poor sleep on marginally chilly nights.

- Wear a beanie to sleep.

- Wear extra layers or all your layers to sleep.

- Fill dead space in your sleeping bag with extra layers, your shelter, or your food bag, especially the foot box and along the zipper of your sleeping bag to prevent drafts.

- Slip the foot box of your sleeping bag into your backpack for an extra layer.

- Tighten down the mummy area of your sleeping bag to prevent drafts.

- Sleep with your sleeping bag upside down so that the mummy part of your bag covers your face. The hot air from your breath can help keep you warm. In moist climates you don't want to do this because the moisture will decrease the loft and insulation of your sleeping bag.

- Don't sleep somewhere where your sleeping bag will pick up dew or condensation.

- Set up your tent or shelter. If you are using a tarp, set it up low to help keep the heat in. A tent can add 10 degrees to your sleep system.

- A bivy sack can also add 5 to 10 degrees of warmth to your sleep system.

- Put two layers of socks on if you have extras.

- Sleep on your side. If necessary, put your head inside your sleeping bag and tuck the mummy hood into the bag to "seal" it and completely prevent drafts.

- Boil water and put it in your water bottle. Making sure the lid is on tight, put the bottle in your sleeping bag and between your legs to help keep you warm.

- Eat something. Give your body fuel for the furnace. I find that a couple scoops of peanut butter do wonders.

- Slip on a pair of gloves.

- Do some push-ups, jumping jacks, or quick calisthenics to warm your body.

- Use your pack liner to create a vapor barrier for your foot box by putting your feet into the pack liner and then into your sleeping bag.

- Find a sleeping area that is protected from the wind, or sleep with your feet on the windward side.

Deal with the Elements without a Lot of Equipment

Despite minimal weight and supplies, it is critical to be prepared for situations you might encounter. Before you head out on your trip, planning ties directly into your preparations and what gear you will need. Good planning allows you to carry minimal equipment while being comfortable and performing at a high level.

Wet and Cold

Some of the most difficult hiking conditions to deal with are wet and cold environments. After persistent rains, you can be soaked to the bone no matter what you are wearing. Add in a chilly wind and a long day of hiking, and you are bound to be chilled to the core. You must be able to set up your shelter easily and without thinking twice. Practice will help you get comfortable and have it become second nature. If your guylines are too thin, they can be hard to tie if your hands are numb. Keep this in mind when prepping your gear and also when taking down your shelter the following morning. Unwanted knots are more than a nuisance when you are fumbling with them, exhausted at

A whiteout at 17,000 feet in Nepal is a good test of my cold weather layering system. You can tell it was chilly since I had two hoods up and my overmitts on. After the uphill to the pass I added my Thermawrap. Pepper's overmitts are stashed in an outside pocket so he can easily grab them.

the end of a long day, and dreaming of crawling into your sleeping bag.

It is also crucial to pack so that you know your sleeping bag will be dry at the end of the day. I pack my sleeping bag and dry gear inside a trash compactor bag inside my pack. I then tuck in the top of the bag to create a seal and waterproof the contents of my pack.

With minimal clothing at my disposal, I have developed a layering system that works well for me; it weighs less than a liter of water and packs down almost as small. If I am in a wet area and in a season that can have cold temperatures, I will often carry or wear the following:

- MontBell Versalite rain pants

- MontBell Versalite rain jacket

- MontBell Thermawrap
- MontBell Wind Parka or Anorak
- MontBell Wind Pants
- Icebreaker merino wool half-zip long-sleeved shirt
- Fleece gloves
- Icebreaker merino wool beanie
- MontBell U.L. Down Inner Jacket
- Mountain Laurel Designs overmitts

My layering system has evolved over time, but I love the versatility this system gives me. I feel completely comfortable heading into any shoulder-season camping situation with this gear. In the middle of summer, I will cull a few items from this list. If it is cold and raining or snowing, I typically will start by wearing my rain jacket over my base layer.

If I am still chilly or getting cold, I will add layers in this order:

1. The wind jacket underneath my rain jacket.
2. The Thermawrap jacket underneath the wind jacket. This allows me to wear the hood of the wind jacket underneath my rain jacket's hood for an additional layer on my head. I will also wear fleece gloves and overmitts on my hands.
3. The wind pants underneath my rain pants.

Whenever it is raining or snowing, I keep my hood up on my rain jacket to prevent water from entering at the collar and soaking my base layers. If I need to shed a layer because I am getting warm, I will take off the Thermawrap while maintaining my waterproof layers. The merino wool base layer stays warmer when it is wet than most other fabrics, and the overmitts help keep my hands warm and dry. *I save my down jacket as an additional layer for camp.* If I am cold and soaked to the bone, I can strip off my wet layers, throw my jacket on, and then crawl into my sleeping bag. This layering system is my go-to system for most cold and wet conditions. If the bad weather persists for days, I can maintain the same layering system, because the synthetic Thermawrap and merino layers continue to insulate when they are wet. When I get up in the morning, I put the wet layers back on since I will be hiking and generating body heat once I get moving. It is initially painful putting on the wet layers but after a few seconds you get used to them. Make sure to strip off the wet layers as soon as you stop hiking for the day and have set up your shelter.

〉〉〉 TIP: Keep food and snacks handy on cold, rainy days. You must fuel your body even though you don't want to stop. Take short breaks and chow down some food, and then move on before you get too cold. Since you can't take extended breaks, just stop earlier at the end of the day.

Adventuring with Your Dog

Dogs are great companions on a hike, but things that are tough or challenging for us can be easy for them and vice versa. To a Chihuahua, for example, a 3-foot rock face that you can easily step up can look like the North Face of the Eiger. Also, it could take a person more than five million steps to cover the Appalachian Trail (AT) from Georgia to Maine, possibly double that for a dog. On the other hand, a dog has four legs.

When hiking in the wilderness with your dog, you have an added responsibility. Test things out and see how the two of you interact before setting off on a big hike. It's important to know your pet's limitations and to read his signs of fatigue and pain, since he can't just shout out and tell you

Four legs can sometimes be better than two. Yoni often thinks snow slopes are no problem, while I struggle to stay upright. In this photo I'm "edging" in with the outside of my right foot to dig into the snow and create a platform to use. Good snow conditions can make steep terrain easier to deal with and cover up tedious talus slopes.

that he's exhausted. Also make sure that all the areas where you're going allow pets. For instance, most US national parks don't allow pets on their trail systems, but check anyway; there are exceptions.

The Main Challenges of Hiking with a Dog and How I Approach Them

Food: Many dogs need double their normal food intake on strenuous or long-distance hikes. You'll learn how much food your dog needs as he or she hikes with you. Yoni eats about two pounds of food per day on a long-distance hike. She weighs about sixty-five pounds. Keep in mind how you binge eat when you get to town after hiking all day. These calories are crucial for you. The same is true for your dog. When we get to town, I feed Yoni as much as possible, but only dog food! I give her multiple cans of dog food on top of her dry food so that she really chows down. I also feed her puppy food on the trail because it has higher calorie content, and I often add a tablespoon or two of vegetable oil to her food for extra calories.

The contents of Yoni's backpack consist of two trash compactor bags, a 3-foot piece of webbing, a PVC-coated dog bowl, and her dog food. A trash compactor bag is used to line each saddlebag before I put the dog food in. This helps to make it easier to balance the load evenly in the saddlebags so the pack sits correctly; a tuck or roll at the top of the trash bag prevents the dog food from getting wet inside the dog pack. The bowl, which enables me to measure her portions, is used mainly for feeding. The PVC coating prevents absorption of oil so the bowl is less likely to smell rank after a lot of use. Occasionally it will also be used for water if there is not a water source around. I use the webbing to tie Yoni to a tree at night or during breaks. She knows when she is tied up that it is time to rest.

Make sure not to overload your dog's pack. I will only pack four or five days of food, at most fourteen pounds, in Yoni's pack. That is about one-fifth of her body weight. On any stretch over five days, I will carry the remaining food and serve her that food first. Dogs can carry more than one-fifth of their body weight, but I choose not to burden her too much, especially since we are repeatedly doing high mileage days. I wouldn't recommend placing more than one-fourth of your dog's body weight into their pack. Also keep in mind that it is imperative to acclimate your dog slowly to the weight. If your first trip is planned for four or five days then you must get your dog used to the pack and weight during training trips. Build up in weight just as you would with your daily mileage.

Water: I hardly ever carry water for Yoni unless I know we're facing a waterless stretch that's over 15 miles and it's really hot out. From being on the trail so much, Yoni has learned she needs to "camel up" at all water sources and now does so naturally. If you're just starting hiking with your dog, don't anticipate he or she will understand that right away; start out by carrying a little extra water for him, and as he no longer needs it, reduce and then eliminate the extra water—if you can. If you're worried your dog's not getting enough water, carry some extra until both of you are used to what she will need. On a lot of trails, such as the AT or the Long Trail, you probably won't have to carry water because there are plenty of water sources. They're generally spaced out at no more than every 7 miles.

I've heard that dogs can get giardia, but I have never seen a dog experience it. I've never treated Yoni's water, and she's had some pretty nasty water. It's up to you if you want to treat your dog's water. It's time-consuming, and when you get to a water crossing, it's hard to stop your dog from drinking when she is thirsty. Still, if Yoni's trying to drink from a foul cattle reservoir and I know there is better water source not far ahead, I'll try to keep her from drinking that water. I'm fussier about not letting her drink from puddles on roadways. She could be ingesting oils, rubber, transmission fluid, glycol, or who knows what else.

>>> TIP: If you're worried about dehydration and want to carry extra stuff for your dog, they make a powdered electrolyte mix for dogs that you can add to the water you put in their bowl. I've used this a couple of times while traveling through the desert, and it seemed to work well. You can also add some Pedialyte to your dog's diet if you want to add electrolytes. Check with your vet for the amounts to use, based on your dog's weight.

River crossings: One issue you'll face with a dog is river crossings. Most dogs aren't very good at moving through swift water, so don't let them fend for themselves on tough crossings. When crossing a river with Yoni, I usually hold her collar and leash in my hand, keeping her downstream. This way she won't take me out if she loses control, and I'll help pull her across as she tries to swim. Sometimes I may even remove her dog pack and strap it onto my pack or toss it to the other side. I do this for any big river crossing, but I'll let her splash through smaller streams and calm rivers.

Snow: Snowdrifts and snowfields shouldn't be an issue for most dogs, since they have lower centers of gravity. Dogs aren't the best on ice. It's like watching them try to run on a wood floor. Be careful on slopes prone to avalanche. Don't let your dog loose in such areas; he could make the situation dangerous for both of you—and anyone else around.

Other Small Hassles: The backcountry is littered with fences, which can present a minor challenge. The ladders and A-frames over fences and electric fences on the AT are a hassle, but they're not a big deal. When steps are too narrow for Yoni to climb, I sometimes have to pick her up and carry her over.

The Continental Divide Trail (CDT) is full of barbed-wire fences without crossings or gates. In such situations I raise the bottom of the fence as high as possible and have Yoni crawl underneath. Then I scramble over the top and inevitably rip my shorts.

First Aid: Many people are worried about their dog getting injured. Despite all the miles Yoni and I have traveled together, we haven't had many first-aid issues. But there are countless problems you could face, so it is important to keep potential issues in mind.

- It is crucial to break your dog in slowly to high mileage, be wary of hot days, and don't overpack her pack.

- Gravel and paved roads can be hard on a dog's paws. Blacktop can be scorching on a warm, sunny day.

- Foxtails can burrow into a dog's skin.

- Ticks can be abundant in certain areas.

- Spring snow (called corn), granite, and lava rocks can be abrasive on a dog's paws.

Certain human first-aid remedies will also work for dogs. For instance, Neosporin is OK to put on cuts; just make sure she doesn't ingest it. Dogs can also have aspirin. But before you start giving your dog aspirin, ask your vet how much aspirin is appropriate. It can help with pain relief and injuries—same as you—but be careful to limit your dog's ambitions. If your dog thinks she is feeling better, she may try to be gung-ho, which can cause further injury.

When hiking in tick country, check your dog's body for ticks regularly. You may also consider using a Frontline-like chemical to help ward off ticks.

Companies also make foot pad creams to protect your dog's pads from cracking or to prevent snow from accumulating on his feet. If both of you are hiking through the snow, and your dog's not wearing booties, consider a protective cream. One of these products is called "Musher's Secret."

Leashes: Even if your dog is good off-leash, keep her on-leash. This is a rule in most areas for good reasons. It's safer for your dog and safer for wildlife, it reduces the impact on wildlife and plant life, and it's more respectful to other visitors. All in all, keeping your dog on a leash is the single biggest thing you can do to prevent a lot of problems and injuries.

It also prevents "dog syndrome," where the dog actually walks at least twice the distance you walk because he wanders around to check everything out. If both of you are putting in high mileage on a regular basis, you definitely want to prevent this, because he can get dog-tired, drained, and burnt out from the trek quickly, which will slow you down considerably.

Walking with a leash and trekking poles can be hard at first; with a little practice both you and your dog can get used to it. Play around with different leash lengths to provide more or less room. But remember that leashes in most places are restricted to no more than 6 feet long.

Another option: Some people rig their dog leash with a carabiner and attach it to their waist belt. That way they don't have to hold the leash all day and can use their trekking poles freely. Some leashes, usually designed for running but certainly suitable for hiking, wrap around your waist, also keeping your hands free.

>>> TIP: There are other reasons to keep your dog on a leash. When she is wearing a dog pack, the leash loop on the back keeps the pack centered on her back so that it doesn't slide down toward or even over her head on downhills, nor will it rub the back of her front legs. Also, if your dog runs through woods unleashed, there's a decent chance that he could lose his pack and all his food. Or he could get tangled up with his pack in some bushes. Then you have to hope you can find the pack. If you can't find it, you'll be up a creek for the remainder of the section or have to cut the trip short.

Need-to-Know Knots

You don't need to know many knots for basic hiking and backpacking. But knowing a few can really come in handy for things like setting up your shelter or hanging your food bag. When your hands are cold, they lose dexterity, so simple knots to set up your shelter at the end of a cold, wet day can make a big difference.

If you're on a trip where you'll be doing some ice or rock climbing or other technical moves, you'll need to know more knots than these.

Slipknot: This is one of the easiest and handiest. It makes it easy to set up and break down your shelter quickly, even when it's raining and/or your hands are cold. My typical version of the slipknot is actually called a granny knot. I tie a slipknot after I do what is called a starting knot, the initial step in tying your shoelaces. This helps to lock the cord before I tie the slipknot, while also allowing the knot to come undone smoothly, easily, and without knotting.

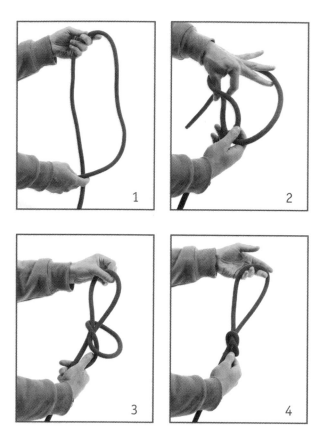

Clove hitch: A clove hitch is helpful for tying cord to your shelter's stakes, because you can tension the cord by pulling on the knot, getting it really tight. When you pull up the stake, you can pop the knot out easily, preventing any unwanted knots in your cord.

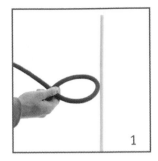

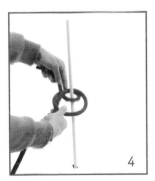

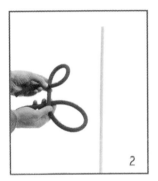

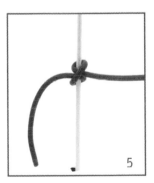

Trauma's simple trucker's hitch: A trucker's hitch is used to tension a rope to make the rope really tight. I use a slipknot as the leverage spot instead of the typical trucker's hitch. This helps you break down your shelter fast and keeps the rope or cord from developing kinks and knots that are hard to undo.

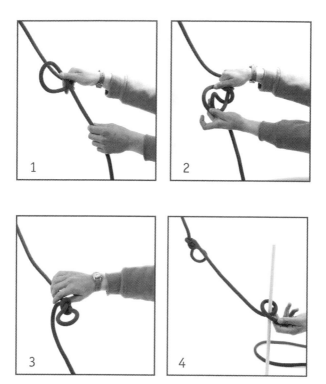

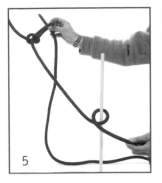

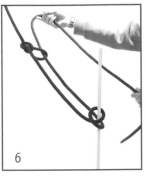

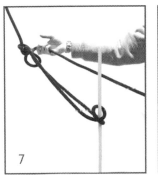

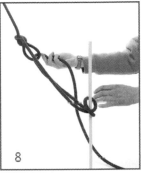

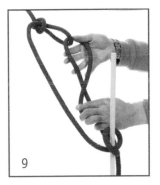

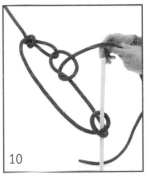

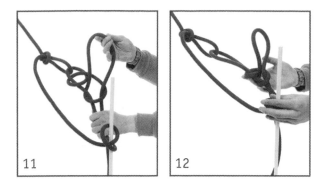

How to Identify Animal Tracks and Other Signs of Wildlife

You're likely to see a lot of animal tracks in the backcountry. When I see tracks, I love trying to piece together what was going on when they were made.

Knowing animal tracks can also help you understand what threats may be around and can tell you what you're likely to see as you are hiking and where not to camp. For instance, they can tell you that a bear or a skunk recently passed where you're walking. They can also tell you that you are about to come upon a herd of deer or caribou or that the spot where you are thinking about camping has been frequented by bears.

Many regional animal guidebooks are available. They'll show you animal tracks, markings, and scat. I wouldn't recommend carrying a field guide unless you plan to read it during downtime. You can purchase guide cards or pamphlets, which are lighter and provide similar information but with a lot less reading and weight. Reading this section will give you general background on what you're seeing.

Rodents: Rodent—rats, mice, marmots, etc.—tracks usually have four toes in the front and five in the rear. They will usually show claw marks. If it's muddy, tracks may show up differently, and heavier rodents such as porcupines and beavers may leave tracks with five toes on the front as well. Normally the three main toes will face forward and the outermost toes will splay to the sides.

Canines: The tale of canines—foxes, coyotes, wolves, and dogs—in North America is told by a couple of markers. Both their front and back paws leave tracks with four toes. Most wild canines leave tracks in straight lines, with the rear foot landing in or near the front foot of the same side. Domestic dogs usually leave a more wandering path and have less of a tendency for their back feet to land in their front feet's prints. Canine toes have an oval shape and a less-obvious heel pad than felines. You're also likely to see nail marks.

Felines: Felines—bobcats, lynxes, ocelots, mountain lions, etc.—leave tracks with four toes on each foot. They have a more-pronounced heel pad than canines. In North America you won't see claw marks. Mountain lions, bobcats, and lynxes all have retractable claws that they can't extend as they walk or run. Felines' footprints are more rounded than canines.

Weasels: Weasels—minks, badgers, wolverines, pine martens, fishers, otters, etc.—leave tracks with five toes on every foot. Their footpad leaves an upside-down V-shape. Claw marks are visible but not as distinct as those of canines. Back feet land close to the front feet because these animals have a leaping gait.

Ungulates (deer and other hoofed animals): Ungulates— deer, moose, elk, caribou, etc.—have cloven hooves that leave a two-toe mark. The main differences between the tracks are their shape and size. In addition, ungulates leave pellet-like scat. Deer leave the smallest pellets and moose the largest.

Bears: Bear tracks are distinct from other North American wildlife. Their feet leave tracks with five toes on the front and back. The back paw prints include a large pad.

TRACK PATTERN

WHITE-TAILED DEER
ABOUT 2½"-3"

MOOSE
ABOUT 4½"-5½"

HEEL / FRONT
DOG
2⅛"- 4"

HEEL 2⅛" / FRONT 2½"
COYOTE

- TRACKS NOT TO SCALE -
TRACKS WILL SHOW VARIATION DEPENDING UPON GROUND CONDITIONS

CROW
2½"

TURKEY
4"

RUFFED GROUSE
2"

TRACK PATTERN

WEASEL
½"- 1"

FISHER
2¼"

FRONT 1" / HEEL 4" — COTTONTAIL RABBIT

HEEL / FRONT
BOBCAT
2"

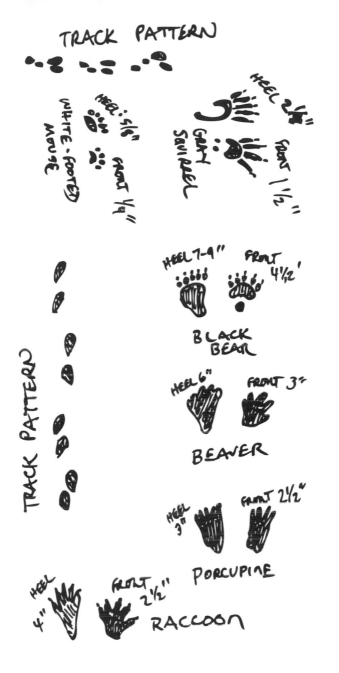

TRACK PATTERN

WHITE-FOOTED MOUSE
HEEL 5/8"
FRONT 1/4"

GRAY SQUIRREL
HEEL 2½"
FRONT 1½"

TRACK PATTERN

HEEL 7-9" FRONT 4½'
BLACK BEAR

HEEL 6" FRONT 3"
BEAVER

HEEL 3" FRONT 2½"
PORCUPINE

HEEL 4" FRONT 2½"
RACCOON

Their scat is in large piles. Bears also scratch tree bark and can leave deep scratch marks on trees. Pay attention to all these indicators, and don't camp in an area with a lot of freshly scratched trees or bear prints.

Raccoons: Raccoons leave tracks with five toes on the front and back. Their tracks look like a small human hand.

Skunks: Similar to the weasel family of prints, skunks leave tracks with five toes on each foot, with large claws in front of the toe imprints.

Rabbits: Rabbits leave tracks with four toes on all feet but no sign of a heel pad. The impressions from the back feet are larger than the front.

Predicting the Weather

When you are in the backcountry, it is always helpful to know what weather may be heading your way even though you don't have access to the Weather Channel. Many small details can help you predict the weather. A barometer with your watch or GPS unit can tell you when the barometric pressure is changing. Increasing pressure usually means better weather; decreasing pressure means the opposite.

>>> TIP: Clear night skies can mean a cold night or two—especially right after a storm passes. The coldest temperatures occur on clear nights.

I am sure you have seen professional meteorologists blow the forecast countless times. It's impossible to know exactly what will happen, but if you're educated about weather indicators and prepared for weather conditions you're likely to encounter, you'll be a lot better off. It's good to pay attention to patterns, such as the wind's direction and the shape and movements of the clouds.

Clouds: When high-level cirrus clouds—those high, wispy clouds or streaks—are building, it means a storm can be heading your way within 48 to 72 hours. Lenticular clouds echoing a peak as they rise into the sky—like the profile of a lens—also may signify that a storm is headed in your direction within that same time frame. A blanket of clouds and spindrift can mean high wind on the peaks.

The march of the storm goes like this:

1. The cirrus clouds come in.
2. They're followed by cirrocumulus clouds—small, puffy clouds that can be rows or ripples.
3. Next are the cirrostratus clouds that cover large areas.
4. They're followed by altostratus—smoky midlevel clouds—and nimbostratus clouds bring the precipitation.

Early morning clouds in the High Sierras forecast an ominous day ahead. Often mountain ranges, especially the High Sierras, go through cycles. Watch for patterns. Sometimes they are 3–5 day cycles and other times 5–7 days. The first day or two will be sunny and bluebird. Then cumulus clouds will start to build a little in the afternoon. A few days later the cumulus clouds are building into full-blown thunderheads, sometimes giving way to afternoon thunderstorms. Ultimately the clouds might simmer down but won't completely disappear by the next morning. This can give the storms a foundation and an early start to pop. Once they have run this course then the cycle often starts over.

Building cumulus clouds over the higher peaks on the side of the valley, caused by warming air and uplifting from the orographics.

Friendly, puffy cumulus clouds can quickly turn angry in the Rockies.

Keep an eye on cumulus clouds. These might be nice, puffy, cottony clouds like those shown at the beginning of *The Simpsons*. But these clouds can quickly turn into nasty cumulonimbus clouds, the breeding grounds of fierce thunderstorms and other violent bursts of weather. In the Rockies these thunderstorms can build from friendly cumulus clouds in minutes. On the AT, a warm, humid day can quickly turn into a torrential downpour and thunderstorm.

If the top of a cumulonimbus cloud has grown so high that it has flattened and spread out into an anvil shape, it is most likely raining very heavily, or even hailing, with thunder and lightning, beneath the cloud. Monitor its direction and path, because you could be in for a soaker.

Wind: Wind direction also plays a major role in predicting the weather. If you understand weather patterns, you know that in the Northern Hemisphere, winds around a low-pressure area circle counterclockwise. Not to get too deep into meteorology, but low-pressure areas have warm fronts and cold fronts. The warm fronts typically have steadier, more persistent rains. The cold fronts typically have heavier bursts or thunderstorms. Temperatures can quickly plummet behind a passing cold front. Winds can tell you if a storm is passing, what stage of the storm you may be in, and what the temperatures are likely to do. For example, if you're hiking in the Sierra Nevada and winds start coming from the south or southwest, a storm might be coming in. If you're hiking in New England and the winds start coming from the north or northwest, temperatures are probably going to get colder.

Lightning: Lightning is one of the major weather concerns on a lot of trails in the United States. Thunder happens because lightning forces air in a cloud to rapidly expand and contract, and that movement creates the sonic wave of thunder. Keep in mind that all thunderstorms have lightning, even though it might be cloud-to-cloud lightning and not visible to you.

>>> TIP: If you're in an area like the Rockies, known for afternoon lightning and thunderstorms in summer, and know you have to travel on exposed ridges, get going early in the morning. Get through alpine areas and exposed ridges before storms hit. An early start to the day is called an "alpine start" for just these reasons!

Lightning is no joke. When you hear thunder or see lightning, it's time to get off high ground. Seek cover in a forested area or low spot, but don't hide under the tallest tree around. Sit on your sleeping pad; it helps insulate you from the ground. Electrical current can travel through the ground if lightning strikes nearby.

>>> TIP: Be extra careful if you see lightning in the desert; it can mean heavy rains. When you've seen lightning, don't camp or get caught in slot canyons, washes, or other potential water paths. It might not even be raining where you are, but rains from far away can build to a wall of water coming through a canyon within minutes. Keep in mind that it can take hours after a rain for a waterway to reach its maximum level. You might not be free and clear just because the rain stopped.

WHEN THINGS TAKE A TURN FOR THE WORST

What to Do When a Thunderstorm Approaches

Run for cover!

Well, not really. I am sure you have heard rules from your mother since you were young: Head for cover; don't go under a tree; don't go to an open area. A lot of this is common sense, but I don't completely agree with some of this advice.

Depending on the situation, I might seek cover in a thunderstorm, but mostly for the goal of staying dry. Sometimes I stop and set up my tarp. Or if I am on the Appalachian Trail, I might run to the next shelter and wait it out. The beauty of this approach is that often a thunderstorm will glide past within an hour or two and leave beautiful hiking conditions and cooler air in its wake. As the storm approaches, I try to judge how fast the clouds are moving so that I know how long I have until the storm starts and roughly how fast the cell may be moving.

Setting up camp in a safe spot before the thunderstorm rolls in. Look for areas with good soil drainage and with trees that are taller than your shelter. Thunderstorms can drop large amounts of rain in a short time and lead to running or pooling water where you least expect it.

I'll hike right through thunderstorms if I am below tree line. When I am above tree line or in open areas, I have to make exceptions. Here are my rules of thumb:

- I seek lower ground or get below tree line; then I often continue hiking through the storm.

- When I can't get off an exposed area, I set up my shelter below the ridgeline or in a low spot. I look for something semi-protected. Then I blow up my sleeping pad or roll out my foam mattress and sit on it cross-legged so that I don't touch the ground directly. This can help diffuse a lightning strike by not being grounded. Sometimes when I set up my shelter, I will also get into my sleeping bag. I'll read a book and wait for the storm to pass. Remember: Five Mississippi's said between lightning and thunder equals 1 mile away of the lightning strike. When you see a flash of lightning in the distance, start counting the seconds until you hear thunder. It depends on your altitude, but sound generally travels at 1 mile every 5 seconds. If you hear thunder 20 seconds after seeing lightning, the lightning is 4 miles away. Keep tabs on this. It'll let you know whether the storm is getting closer to you or farther away. If you're comfortable where you're at, sit and wait it out. Or just hike through it, getting out of alpine regions as quickly as possible.

The temperature can drop a lot as the air gets saturated with moisture and when the storm front passes.

Keep in mind that sometimes in the high country or under the right, or maybe I should say wrong, conditions, thunderstorms can sit in one spot or redevelop over a certain area. It's not always one and done!

How to Escape a Lion . . . or Any Animal (More Likely You'll Be Dealing with Rodents and Other Miscellaneous Troublemakers)

People are always asking me, "What do you do about the animals? Are bears and mountain lions really dangerous? Do you carry a gun?" Honestly, I don't worry much about the wildlife. Typically wild animals are more scared of us than we are of them. They try to avoid us as much as possible and don't want to waste energy on people because they know we are not food.

〉〉〉 TIP: If local regulations permit, I try to camp in low-impact fashion. I often camp in impacted areas or frequently camped spots. However, if I am concerned about animals or bears, I will often cook dinner at least 1 mile before reaching my camping destination. Other times I try to camp in infrequently used areas, where animals that associate people and food will not bother looking. When I camp in these locations I leave them as I found them so that I don't create an additional impacted camping site.

An unexpected and unwelcome visit from a lion while hiking through Africa. I think the single biggest reason I am still alive is because I did not run from the lion and trigger its natural chasing and hunting instincts.

Keep in mind that this theory holds true for most areas, except for national parks. In these protected areas, we have changed the balance of nature by banning hunting and concentrating human use. There are still tourists who feed the animals, intentionally or unintentionally. Even small crumbs left over in campsites can lead to behavioral changes in animals. Over time this has altered the natural fear of the animals and caused them to associate humans with food. As a result in some places, like Yosemite National Park, bears became habituated and a bit out of control. Proper food storage, including bear canisters, is now required. In general, I am still more concerned about mice eating my food (like in the shelters along the Appalachian Trail) than about any big, scary, predatory animal—despite the lion, elephant, leopard, mountain lion, and grizzly encounters I have experienced.

How to Deal with a Big, Scary Animal

1. Don't run!!!! Never run! Hold your ground. Many predators naturally want to chase and kill something that runs from them. Don't let them associate you with the thrill of the hunt.

2. Raise your arms. Make your presence known. It's possible that you walked around a corner and surprised the animal. Start talking to it, and then keep raising your voice until you are yelling at the animal as loud as you can.

3. If the animal doesn't turn around and start leaving, continue yelling, bang your trekking poles together, and start picking up and tossing rocks near the animal. Don't try to hit it; just fire warning shots.

4. If it still isn't leaving, start backing away slowly, without turning your back on the animal. Continue all of your scare tactics from the previous step as you slowly back away. If you are on a trail, it can sometimes help to walk off the trail, because animals also use the trails to travel.

When Things Take a Turn for the Worst

Your tactics are not working, and the animal is now charging! Continue holding your ground. Yell, scream, bang your trekking poles, raise your arms and wave them. Do whatever you can to appear loud and large. Often animals will bluff charge in order to try to show their dominance and that this is their territory. If the animal starts to act aggressively, you need to start fighting back. Throw rocks. Jab it with sticks or your trekking poles in its eyes, ears, nose, and mouth. If the animal takes you down to the ground, you need to change plans. Ditch your backpack and start playing dead. Lie face down on the ground with your hands over the back of your neck and your elbows splayed to side. This will protect your head, neck, and vital organs, while also providing stability so that the animal cannot easily roll you over. At this point the animal may get bored with you and check out your backpack, then decide to move on. Often if these circumstances happen the animal is just curious or displaying territorial tendencies. If the animal continues to pursue you in a fierce and predatory way, you need to start fighting back and try poking it in the eyes as much as you can. These are your best lines of defense.

>>> TIP: Mother bears can be ornery when you get between them and their cubs. This is a special circumstance in which I would NOT recommend holding your ground. As soon as you realize that you are between a mother bear and her cubs, you need to start backing away or moving out from between them. Never climb a tree! Most black bears, and all cubs, can climb trees. Also, they are definitely strong enough to make the tree sway dangerously or even knock some trees down.

How to Deal with Snakes and Other Biting Animals and Insects

Snakes: Many people are scared of snakes, particularly rattlesnakes, but they're relatively easy to avoid. Pay attention during the day, particularly when you get to an open rocky area. Snakes love to sun themselves during the day on rocks and in open areas. That's also when they have the energy to strike.

If you hear a rattle or see a snake, don't keep moving toward the snake or antagonize it. Most snakebites are on people's hands and wrists, likely because they antagonize the snakes. Give the snake some berth; walk around it and you'll be fine. Most snakes, especially in the United States, aren't aggressive and don't want to bite you. They know you are too big to be food, so they would rather not waste the energy. It's a different story if you antagonize them or get too close.

Most rattlesnake bites are dry bites, bites that don't inject venom. Even rattlesnake bites with venom are rarely deadly, except for in kids and elderly people. Juvenile rattlesnakes are the deadliest because they can't control the amount of venom they inject. Adult rattlesnakes know that people are too big for them to eat and so won't bother wasting much venom. The rattling noise serves as a warning sign

A rattlesnake ready to strike.

Tarantulas can be found in New Mexico along the CDT.

Another rattlesnake.

A scorpion in Utah.

You will first hear the rattle and then maybe a hiss. Rattlesnakes usually coil up like this before they strike. Step back and give it a wide berth. As you can see in both rattlesnake pictures, the snakes were sunning themselves when I came up on them. They are getting defensive because I approached them fast and directly since they were on or right next to the trail.

The worst of all biting things... mosquitoes. This pile is from only 5 minutes of swatting!

that you are getting close. Just obey the alert and you won't have any issues.

Coral snakes have very toxic venom, but many bites are also dry bites. Remember: "Red on yellow, kill a fellow. Red on black, venom lack." There are many types of snakes that are red, yellow, and black. The order of the stripes dictates whether it is a venomous coral snake.

If you do get bit, try to calm down. Less than 10 percent of all snakebite victims die. Rinse the wound. Clean the bite. Apply antiseptic, antihistamine (toothpaste if that's all you have with you), and antibiotic ointment. Remove any tight jewelry or clothing. Immobilize the extremity by applying a compression bandage and an immobilizer. This will help lower the circulation through the area. DO NOT apply a tourniquet or cut off blood flow to the extremity! Make sure the skin distal to the bandage still returns to color after you press on it. Do not remove the bandage once it is applied. If possible, elevate the wound over your heart to slow the spread of venom and to minimize swelling. If you are alone, you must hike out or call for help. If you are with friends, have them carry you out so that you don't stimulate circulation from walking. Seek medical attention as soon as possible.

Use a marker to circle the bite on the patient's skin and make a note of the time. If the area starts swelling, mark additional circles with time notes so that you can monitor the progress of any swelling. This helps doctors understand the severity of the bite. If you can easily identify the snake or make note of its features, size, markings, and color, this information can also help the medical staff.

>>> TIP: If you are camping in rattlesnake country and have set up camp earlier in the day, shake out your sleeping bag before you crawl in at night. It is extremely rare, but the heat of the sleeping bag and a human body can attract a snake.

Scorpions: Scorpion species are widespread and are adapted to live in all climates and continents except Antarctica. They are nocturnal and seek shelter during the day, usually below ground or underneath rocks. They seek these cooler, protected locations to avoid predators. As a result, human interaction is minimal and can usually easily be avoided. If you are in common scorpion environs, be careful when overturning rocks and reaching into rock crannies. It sometimes can be a good idea to turn your shoes upside down before putting them on.

Fatalities from scorpion stings are very rare, although possible in children and elderly individuals. Only 25 out of about 1,750 species of scorpion have venom strong enough to kill a human. However, all scorpions can pierce human skin and leave a painful, unpleasant sting. Most will usually leave redness around the sting. Scorpion stings have quick-acting toxins. Treatment is usually symptomatic, with acetaminophen or ibuprofen, cold compresses (cold water or snow), and, if necessary, transport to advanced medical care.

Spiders: In North America there are three types of venomous spiders: brown recluse (also known as fiddleback), black widows, and tarantulas. All have bites that inject toxins that can lead to neurologic issues or necrosis but are rarely fatal. These spiders all live in dark places and usually in confined areas or corners. They are not aggressive and will typically only bite when provoked. Occasionally they may mistake a human finger for a caterpillar or other food, but this is rare. As a result, backcountry incidents are uncommon.

Out of the spiders that have large enough chelicerae, a spider's mouthparts, to pass through human skin, 98 percent will have no medical consequence. In addition, bacterial infection from spider bites is highly unlikely and occurs at less than 1 percent. Healthy adults have little to worry about. Black widow spiders are among the most toxic, and while their bites can cause very painful muscle spasms and paralysis (usually temporary), they are seldom life threatening. No one in the United States has perished from a black widow bite in more than ten years. Most brown recluse bites are minor, with no toxin released. They can also produce skin lesions and other conditions, including organ damage, but rarely cause fatalities. Tarantulas have large fangs that can inject a lot of venom, but their bites generally only cause localized pain. The hairs on the tarantula can also cause irritation.

Most spider bites are harmless and require no additional treatment. If bitten by a nonvenomous spider, wash the bite with water, take ibuprofen, and ice the area. If bitten by a venomous spider, remain calm. Most bites are self-limiting and will run their course, but it is beneficial to try to properly identify the spider variety, immobilize the limb, remove any constricting jewelry, elevate the limb if possible, and apply cold compresses. If you think a black widow or brown recluse has bitten you, head out and seek medical attention.

Biting insects: A horde of biting insects sucks, literally. I am more bothered by mosquitoes, no-see-ums, blackflies, and other biting insects than by snakes, spiders, and scorpions, since the former are unavoidable and painfully annoying. To keep them away, you can try bug repellent, head nets, or insect-proof clothing. But in some places not even 100% DEET is good enough for complete protection. Covering up can sometimes give you peace of mind when the bugs are really bad.

Some natural bug repellents work when the bugs aren't too bad. But you need to reapply them more frequently than DEET. When the bugs are bad, nothing compares with 100% DEET. However, DEET has its own downsides. It can ruin anything plastic, synthetic fabric, watch crystals, and eyeglass frames, and some people have a negative reaction to it.

Still, sometimes peace of mind is priceless. In the buggiest conditions, it's worth the weight to carry a head net and bug netting for your shelter or a bug-proof tent.

>>> TIP: When applying sunscreen and insect repellent, put the sunscreen on first and let it absorb into your skin for a few minutes and then apply the bug juice. Putting them on in the reverse order will reduce the functionality of each. The sunscreen will alter the smell of the bug dope, and the insect repellent will sit in between your skin and the sunscreen, preventing it from doing its job.

Stinging Insects: You're not likely to encounter bees, wasps, hornets, and yellow jackets often. Stings are painful but relatively harmless for most people. If you are highly allergic, you should talk to your doctor and take appropriate precautions, such as carrying a EpiPen. Otherwise, if you're stung, scrape the stinger out and ice the area. Benadryl can be helpful as an antihistamine. If you don't have that, using toothpaste topically can help—the fluoride will act as an antihistamine.

>>> TIP: Natural insect repellents include tea tree oil—which also can be used as an antibacterial agent—citronella, lemon eucalyptus, rose geranium, pennyroyal, patchouli, neem tree oil, and peppermint (for ants). These are OK for certain situations. When bugs are really biting, DEET is the only repellent that works.

Ticks: Ticks are common on the AT when spring rolls around. Do body checks on any trail, but especially on the AT. Ticks can carry Lyme disease, ehrlichiosis, and Rocky Mountain spotted fever. I once pulled handfuls of ticks off Yoni on the AT, near the Shenandoah Mountains. There were hordes of them—I couldn't pull them off fast enough. Lyme Disease is becoming increasingly common along the AT, and proper diagnosis and early treatment are very important. Still, not all ticks transmit Lyme disease. The culprits are mainly deer ticks; the smaller variety hosts the disease, and the nymphs can be as small as a poppy seed.

Ticks are attracted to warm areas of the body, so check your scalp, ears, armpits, backs of your knees, and groin. It can be helpful to locate and remove ticks quickly. Some medical professionals think your chances of infection increase after the tick has been attached for more than 24 hours. If you find a tick, try to pull it out without squeezing the body too much. Pinch the tick near the head and pull it out. Don't twist. If a red or bull's-eye rash develops around the tick bite, visit a doctor as soon as possible. Other symptoms of Lyme disease include fatigue, joint pain, nausea, headache, and fever. Incubation time is usually one to two weeks but can also be a few days or longer than two weeks. When the red bull's-eye does not develop, many of the symptoms can easily be mistaken as typical hiking maladies. Be cautious. Early administration of antibiotics is very important.

>>> TIP: If you're having trouble getting a tick out, here's a great trick. Put liquid soap on a cotton ball, cover the tick with the cotton ball, and swab it for 15 to 20 seconds. The tick will come out of your skin on its own and be stuck to the cotton ball when you lift it.

How to Identify Poisonous Plants and Treat Reactions

Poison ivy, poison oak, poison sumac, and stinging nettles are fairly common on parts of the AT, Pacific Coast Trail (PCT), and on lots of other hiking trails in the United States. Know what they look like, and do your best to avoid them.

Poison sumac and stinging nettle are a little harder to discern than poison ivy and poison oak, but they are respectively less common and less irritating. Stinging nettles only usually burn for about 15 minutes and don't leave a residual rash, so they are relatively harmless.

Identification

"Leaves of three, let them be" is a good rule of thumb for both poison ivy and poison oak.

Poison Ivy: Three pointed leaflets with smoothed or toothed edges and varying in length from 2 to 4 inches. It can grow as ground cover, a shrub, or a vine. The leaves are often reddish in spring and green in summer. Poison ivy is normally found in forested areas and along the edges of forested and open areas. It also grows in rocky areas and open fields. Typically likes full sunlight and isn't very shade tolerant.

Poison Oak: The plant grows as a shrub or a vine, with leaves shaped like oak leaves in groups of three. The

Poison Oak

underside of the leaf is often lighter than the surface and has tiny hair filaments. The leaves also change color seasonally, from bronze when they are unfolding, to green in spring, to red in fall. It is usually found near running water in damp, semi-shaded areas or bright sun.

Poison Sumac: This is usually a dense shrub or small tree; the leaves grow in pairs, with typically seven to thirteen pairs on a branch. The leaves are always smooth, and small white or gray berries can hang in clusters from the stalk. Leaves also change seasonally and can be green or red.

》》 TIP: If you aren't ultrasensitive to the plants—you don't have an immediate reaction—it's extra helpful to know what the plants look like. I have knowingly but unavoidably touched poison ivy and poison oak many times. I try to find a creek or water source to wash the contact area, hopefully within 30 minutes. If I didn't know what the plants looked like, I could end up with a nasty rash. But by washing soon after, I have avoided the itchy rash, which can bother you for days. This also prevents spreading the urushiol even more.

It's not only poison ivy, oak, and sumac that are dangerous. When bushwhacking, spiny plants like blackberry bushes or yucca and stiff plants like tamarisk and manzanita can be very painful also.

⟩⟩⟩ TIP: It's an old wives' tale that you can spread the rash by scratching it or by breaking blisters. Scratching can make the rash itch even more, but once you wash off the urushiol, you can no longer spread the "poison."

Keep in mind that the urushiol (the plants' irritating oil) is not just on the leaves. It's on all parts of the plants, including the bark, vines, roots, and twigs, and can rub onto your clothing, shoes, or dog and later get onto your skin if it is not washed off. Also, it can be released as smoke and inhaled when the plants are burned.

Out of Food
General Rules for Edible Plants

If you get into a tough situation and run out of food, here are some general guidelines to follow on recognizing edible plants without carrying a guidebook. It doesn't make sense to hunt for game unless you are going to be stationary for a couple of days. You are better off moving toward your next resupply and looking for edible plants, which are

You can see a plant in the legume family in the foreground on the right. Don't be fooled because some legumes are commonly eaten and seen in the supermarket. Most plants in the legume family are not edible and have varying levels of toxicity.

more common and require less time and energy to acquire. Make sure to eat only plants and mushrooms that you can positively identify. I recommend steering clear of mushrooms in an emergency situation. Identifying mushrooms can be difficult and must be precise. There is not much room for experimentation, since some mushrooms are highly toxic.

> *"Leaves of three, let them be. Leaves of four, eat some more."*

To avoid potentially harmful plants, stay away from any wild or unknown plants that have:

- Milky or discolored sap
- Beans, bulbs, or seeds inside a pod
- Three-leaved growth pattern
- Grain heads with black, purple, or pink spurs
- Almond scent in woody parts and leaves
- Dill-, carrot-, parsnip-, or parsley-like foliage
- Spines, hairs, or thorns
- Bitter or soapy taste

If you are trying something new, try small quantities and allow more than 24 hours before eating more. If you are trying to identify potential edible plants, do not ingest more than one unknown plant in a 24-hour period. If you can safely ingest the plant, make sure the plant is abundant enough to be worth your while. Keep in mind that some plants have parts that are edible and other parts that are not.

First Aid with Minimal Supplies

The likelihood of a major injury happening in the backcountry is slim, but you still need to be prepared in case it does happen. Being ready for any circumstance does not mean being overequipped. Most of the time you will be dealing with blisters and other foot problems, sunburn, chafe, or small cuts and bruises. You can use the equipment you have with you to safely remedy most situations, including serious injuries. No need to carry anything extra for those "just in case" situations. Get creative; you should have everything you need, even in a minimalist backpack.

>>> TIP: Improper hygiene on the trail can lead to illnesses from sharing food or even shaking hands. Be careful when sharing food on the trail. Don't let someone dig into your stash of trail mix. Pour it from the bag into his or her hand instead. This can prevent cross-contamination, one of the most common causes of trail illness.

Much first aid is common sense. Remember the basics—RICE: rest, ice, compression, and elevation. This will help to stop bleeding on fresh injuries and help injuries heal quicker.

You never know what you can use for first aid. A Priority Mail sticker from the local post office came in handy when my shoes were rubbing my heel as I walked around town. Cheap, ultralight, and creative first aid!

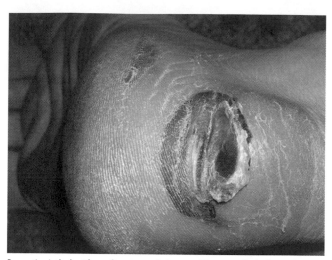

Prevention is the best form of treatment. Before your blisters get this bad, tape them up. They'll heal a lot faster! And remember—don't remove the loose skin.

Sometimes accidents happen. Clean out a cut with fresh clean water. Apply direct pressure to stop the bleeding and cover it to keep it clean.

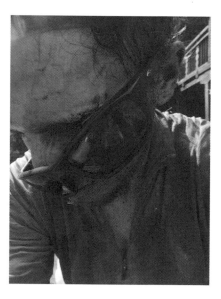

⟩⟩⟩ TIP: Proper immobilization requires splinting above and below the injured joint. If it's an injured long bone area, the joint above and below the injury must be immobilized.

My Minimalist First Aid Kit
- About 3 to 5 feet of duct tape wrapped around my fuel bottle or trekking pole, so I don't have to carry the roll of duct tape
  Uses:
  * Blister protection and prevention
  * Bandages for bleeding, compression wraps, sprains, and injuries
  * Protection against foot chafe or rubbing

- Ibuprofen, about 30 to 50 pills taken out of the bottle and put in a 2-milliliter (2 × 2-inch) or 4-milliliter (4 × 4-inch) self-locking plastic baggie. Unlike acetaminophen (Tylenol), ibuprofen helps alleviate inflammation as well as take care of the pain.
  Uses:
  * pain relief
  * anti-inflammatory

- Needle
  Uses:
  * popping blisters

- Small knife, scissors, or nail clippers
  Uses:
  * foot care
  * cutting nails and ingrown toenails
  * also used for food preparation

- If hiking internationally in a second- or third-world country, take a prescription and over-the-counter drug

kit including Imodium, ciprofloxacin, and tinidazole. Possibly also mefloquine if in malaria country.
Uses:
* to prevent and treat possible illnesses in the backcountry

Multipurpose Items:
- Trekking poles
  Uses:
  * splints
  * immobilization
  * crutches

- Base layers, a bandanna, or spare clothes
  Uses:
  * dressings for wounds
  * compression wraps
  * slings, swathes
  * affix to trekking or tent poles for immobilization

- Water bottle, pot, or hydration bladder
  Uses:
  * ice pack (using cold creek water or filling with snow) or a water rinse
  * warm up your body by heating water on the stove and pouring it into your pot or water bottle

- Sleeping pad
  Uses:
  * splint, immobilization

>>> TIP: If you use a chemical water treatment, it can double as a hand sanitizer, especially before dealing with broken skin. Just pour some Aquamira- or iodine-treated water over your hands or place a small dose of the chemical mix on your hands and rub them like applying hand sanitizer.

Minor injuries can be majorly debilitating on a hike. Here are some likely/potential injuries and how to care for them.

Foot care: It is important to look after your feet. After all, they're in constant contact with the ground.

- Rest your feet whenever possible. Elevate your feet and legs to encourage good circulation and reduce swelling.

- Ventilate and dry your feet out by removing your shoes and socks when you rest, day or night. At the same time, shake dirt and gravel out of them and remove their insoles so they can dry out too. If it's hot, get in a stream and soak your feet and legs.

- When you put your socks on, make sure they're free of debris and wrinkles. Either can cause blisters. Also, keeping your socks clean and rinsing them out occasionally will help prevent them from getting gritty and help prevent rubbing and other foot problems.

- Cracked feet are caused by dry conditions—often from hiking in sandals. If this is the case for you, wearing socks with your sandals will keep your feet from drying out as much. If necessary, clean the crack in your foot out and use superglue to help hold the crack together so that it can heal. If you see cracks developing, pick up superglue at your next resupply. I no longer hike in sandals because of this.

>>> TIP: If it's convenient and you have time, soak your feet and legs in a creek or lake at the end of the day. It feels great and can help with injury recovery and prevention. It's like icing your legs. Bonus: It helps keep your sleeping bag clean!

>>> **TIP:** If you think you have an ingrown toenail, cut a V-shaped notch in the middle of the toenail. It can alleviate pressure on the side of the nail and help the ingrown part the nail grow out as the toenail grows in.

Blisters: When dealing with blisters, be proactive. Try to tape them as soon as you feel a hot spot developing. Or if you have a common blister location, consider dressing it before you begin. By catching things early, you can prevent a lot of agony in the long run.

Treatment: Place a small piece of duct tape shiny-side up against a larger piece's sticky side so the tape won't stick to the injury. When you remove the tape, you will not do any additional damage or rip off the loose skin. Peel the tape off each night when you are done hiking so the cut or blister has time to dry and harden. If you have a blister that hasn't popped, lance it in the evening when you are done hiking. Use a lighter to sterilize the needle. Poke the needle into the blister from un-blistered skin adjacent to the blister. Choose a fairly protected spot or one that gets the least amount of friction or movement in your shoes. Don't pop the blister directly, and do not peel off the loose skin. That skin will help prevent pain and infection. Cover it with duct tape as mentioned before hiking the next day.

Chafe: Chafe is often a hiker's worst nightmare. It can be debilitating, making it almost too painful to walk. Common areas that chafe are the inner thighs, butt crack, feet, armpits, and back. Women may chafe under their bra line or bust. Moisture, friction, and the buildup of salt crystals from sweat are the root of the problem. The salt crystals then rub skin rough and raw. If you're chafed, you may end up walking like John Wayne.

Treatment: Treat chafe as soon as you notice it, otherwise it can get worse and may even become infected. Wash chafed skin with freshwater, and let it dry completely. Promote airflow to the region to let it dry out, but make sure to keep it clean.

- If your feet or ankles are chafing, change or wash your socks. They may be gritty, causing the chafing.

- Treat the chafed skin by rinsing with clean water to remove dirt, sweat, and built-up salt crystals. Don't rub; this will only abrade and irritate the skin more. Wash your shirt, shorts, socks, or underwear. Then apply petroleum jelly such as Vaseline, Sportslick, or other skin-lubricating products. The treatment will help prevent additional friction, which will give the skin a chance to heal. Even though I don't typically carry any of these antifriction products, I will buy one at my next resupply if I am having any chafe issues.

General Aches and Pains: Most people have aches and pains when they are starting a backpacking trip or a thru-hike. The biggest prevention is training, getting your body used to wearing a weighted backpack and hiking. Stretching in the morning, at breaks, and in the evening helps reduce discomfort and can prevent injuries.

Treatment/Prevention: Don't push your body too hard before it's ready. Build your daily mileage slowly. If you are thru-hiking or otherwise out for a long time, start with a comfortable mileage where you aren't pushing too hard. As your body acclimates to that mileage, add a few more miles some days. For about half a week, hike just the base comfortable mileage on other days. Take a rest day. If you feel good, continue to up the mileage until the higher mileage becomes your base mileage. Repeat the whole process to reach a new level if you can. It can take a month or more to increase your daily base mileage between 5 and 15 miles. Don't increase your mileage too much too fast. I have seen a lot of injuries result from increasing too quickly.

For muscle aches, massage your muscles and take "vitamin I"—ibuprofen; it helps with pain and inflammation.

For joint pain, rest helps the most. Vitamin I can also ease the pain and inflammation. Stop hiking a little earlier in the day to extend your rest time, or hike a few shorter days. You can also elevate the sore joints and ice your joints with cold water. Taking glucosamine and chondroitin pills during a long hike may also aid in the repair of cartilage.

A big factor in joint pain could also be that your pack load is heavy. Ultralight travel helps to remove much of the burden on your body, your joints, and particularly your knees. A pound of weight loss equals four less pounds of pressure on your knees. "The accumulated reduction in knee load for a one-pound loss in weight would be more than 4,800 pounds per mile walked," wrote researcher Stephen P. Messier, PhD, of Wake Forest University in the July 2005 issue of *Arthritis & Rheumatism*. "For people losing 10 pounds, each knee would be subjected to 48,000 pounds less in compressive load per mile walked." Sign me up!

Furthermore, leg pain could be resulting from heavy shoes. If you are wearing hiking boots instead of trail runners, they can add weight and strain to your body. Regarding energy exertion, one pound of weight on your feet equals ten pounds on your back.

>>> TIP: I have seen countless hikers experience knee pain. It can be from any number of things, but often there is an easy solution. Walking or hiking repeatedly can tighten the IT band, which can in turn pull your patella off track and create knee pain. The IT band runs along the outside of your upper leg from your hip down to your knee. A simple remedy is to firmly massage your IT band at night and during breaks. You can also stretch it by doing a lunge-type maneuver where both of your knees are at 90-degree angles and your upper body remains perfectly upright. Hold the position a few seconds and then take a step and repeat it with your other leg. Continue the routine for a minute or so. A physical therapist can tell you additional stretches to target this area.

>>> **TIP:** I use my pack as the lower half of my sleeping pad. This saves weight and elevates my legs while I sleep. This helps prevent inflammation in my feet and legs and keeps my shoes fitting properly, helping to prevent any foot problems.

Altitude Sickness (AMS): People get AMS when they travel to high altitudes. Often they don't even realize what is causing their headache or nausea. Some people start feeling it around 6,000 feet; others won't feel it until around 10,000 feet above sea level. Your reaction largely depends on the elevation you live at and your fitness level.

Initial symptoms of AMS are sluggishness and headaches. If the condition progresses, it can be debilitating and even deadly.

Treatment/Prevention: Controlled acclimatization is the best prevention for AMS. People generally try to ascend about 1,000 meters (3,000 feet) per day. Camp at the new level, and try to acclimatize.

When summiting big peaks like Mount Everest, people acclimatize by spending one night at a higher elevation, then descending and camping at a lower level before ascending higher. That helps their body adjust to the oxygen-starved environs. Some people take acetazolamide (brand name Diamox) to feel better at high altitudes. This can present an additional danger by masking the symptoms of AMS until you are feeling really bad. I recommend acclimatizing properly rather than taking acetazolamide. If you do decide to take acetazolamide, remember to discuss it with your doctor. It is preventative, so ask about starting to take it two to three days before you go to a higher elevation. Acetazolamide is a diuretic, so make sure to hydrate if you are taking it. There have also been some studies indicating gingko biloba as a natural treatment/preventative for AMS.

At lower elevations, staying hydrated, avoiding crazy elevation changes in a short amount of time, and acclimatizing can largely prevent AMS. If you are suffering from altitude sickness, the best thing to do is descend to a lower elevation.

How to Repair or Replace Gear with Limited Materials

A key part of ultralight hiking is being able to adapt to any situation you may encounter. The unexpected is bound to happen, and you must be adaptable enough to come up with a solution with the minimal supplies you have with you. I have fine-tuned my kit so that I know the minimum I will need to avert most situations. Getting creative, since you don't have the kitchen sink with you, is part of the fun of an ultralight kit. My whole repair kit weighs less than two ounces—it also doubles as some of my first-aid needs.

>>> TIP: If you snap a trekking pole, it isn't essential for hiking but can be for setting up your tarp or shelter. Depending on what type of shelter you are using, one or two trekking poles can be necessary to provide structure. If you only need one pole to set up your shelter, you should be fine. If you need both poles (or end up breaking both), here are some options: You can use a tree branch or strap or tie the broken pole to a tree branch each night. You can also extend the pole as far as it allows and then add a rock underneath to increase the height. With some shelters, you also may be able to guy out the spot where the trekking pole would go and tie it off to a tree.

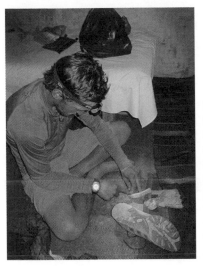

Sometimes you have to get creative to get your gear to your next resupply. In Nepal it was common to see worn-out shoes in the gutters in town and even sometimes in the backcountry. A knife, a little Super Glue or duct tape, and some cobbler skills helped my shoes last the final three days until the end of Nepal.
Photo by Shawn Forry

Many of the field repairs I do will last the life of the product. However, if there is a critical failure, like a shoe blowout, the repair only needs to make it until my next resupply stop, especially on hikes in the United States. This can be anywhere from one day to ten days of hiking (an average of 30 to 300 miles). I can then continue to use my nearly dead shoes or pick up some new ones in town, depending on how the repair is holding up. Although most fixes will last a long time, keep in mind that anything that needs to be repaired only has to perform until the next town stop.

>>> TIP: If you are carrying dental floss, you can use it in place of thread for repairs.

My Simple Repair Kit

- About 3 to 5 feet of duct tape wrapped around my fuel bottle or trekking pole so that I don't have to carry the roll of duct tape
  Uses:
  * Shoe repair
  * First aid (see First Aid section)
  * Tent pole/trekking pole repairs
  * Miscellaneous backpack repairs and other fixes

- About 1 foot of Tenacious Tape (a really sticky clear tape made by Gear Aid that does not leave a residue when removed)
  Uses:
  * Fabric rips
  * Sleeping bag repair
  * Clothing rips
  * Inflatable sleeping pad repairs

- Needle and thread, to fit in a small, 1-inch-tall plastic container
  Uses:
  * Zipper repair
  * Clothing rips
  * Fabric rips

- Most things I carry have dual purposes. For example, I can use the cord from my shelter guylines for a shoelace or a repair.

>>> TIP: When using Tenacious Tape or duct tape, overlap at least 1 inch on both ends of the rip in order to prevent the rip from spreading. When using Tenacious Tape for fabric, sleeping bag, and inflatable sleeping pad repairs, cut the tape with rounded corners. This will prevent the edges from catching on things and result in a longer lasting repair.

Finding Water

Finding water is a life-saving skill. Even when you're not in trouble, you still need to know how to find water.

Always read the legend or key on your map. Most hiking maps will depict seasonal creeks with dashed or dotted lines. On colored maps they're usually blue. On black-and-white maps they might be different from other dashed patterns. However, you can't rely on seasonal creeks as likely water sources. A solid line—again a blue line on colored maps—usually marks permanent creeks, streams, springs, and rivers. Some maps have different symbols for seasonal springs, seeps, and hot springs. Such things are explained in the map legend.

Don't automatically think that the deeper ravines, canyons, or watercourses are most likely to have water. Look for where they originate (lake, spring, or a big cirque with permanent snowfields) and what direction they are facing. In the Northern Hemisphere, north-facing mountain slopes and watercourses are the most likely to hold water because

A pool at the bottom of a pour-off. During times of high flow, the extra force of the water careening off the pour-off creates an impression in the sand or bedrock. This can hold residual water long after the canyon has dried up following rain.

they stay cooler and shadier. The opposite is true in the Southern Hemisphere.

The time of day can play a huge role in a watercourse's flow. A water source fed by snowmelt can swell throughout the day. But under other conditions it can shrink to the point of disappearing. In a desert or sandy terrain and in hot weather, water can quickly evaporate and disappear. I have seen a creek disappear into the sand in a matter of minutes. In these circumstances, water may be available in the morning but not later in the day. If you're likely to face this situation on your hike, consider carrying extra water.

When looking for water, look for certain types or a long line of vegetation, such as willows. Sycamores and willows love water and often live near streams. They also are an indication that water may be close to the surface, even if no water is visible. If you dig into the ground, water may seep and pool in the cavity.

Water is often seasonal in the desert. Most deserts get precipitation in winter. And while they're mostly dry in summer, some deserts get monsoon-level rain in the middle of summer. You may find potholes or holes in sandstone that keep water in them. It's probably not the best-tasting water, but it's water nonetheless. Don't bathe in potholes. Wildlife and microorganisms need these to survive.

Sometimes all you can find is silty water, particularly in desert conditions. In these conditions—especially if you're using a SteriPEN or filter—first use your shirt or a bandanna to help filter out sediment when you fill your water bottle. If you're filling up when you stop for the evening, stand your reservoirs or bottle upright before you go to sleep. That way, any sediment left in the bottle will settle to the bottom overnight and you can drink or pour the water in the morning without getting sediment.

In desert canyons, a dry pour-off or dry waterfall can have a pool of water below. These can last long after the rest of the canyon has dried up.

Cliffed Out

Nobody wants to turn back and lose time. That's definitely one of my pet peeves. I usually try to keep charging forward. I have experienced countless times when the topo map didn't portray the landscape like it really was. Maybe

This cliff band is known as The Waterfall Face. It is a notoriously tricky area near Rabbit Pass in New Zealand and can be impassable in foul weather. Keep in mind some things may be doable in dry conditions, but slippery and dangerous when wet, snowy, or icy. Adjust your plans or route accordingly.

the cliff was less than the contour line intervals or the map just didn't read like it should, or maybe I just messed up and chose a bad route. These are all reasons you could find yourself standing on top of a cliff wondering if there's a doable way down. The single biggest thing to remember here is: Don't go down something you can't get back up!

You can try finding a way down. Sometimes it works and sometimes it doesn't. If it isn't a sheer cliff, then it is often doable. You can often tell this by the type of rocks you are looking at and the nature of the cliff. Does the cliff look like El Capitan, or is it a blocky mix of sandstone? If the cliff is blocky and not a continuous, unbroken rock face, there can often be a way to pick your way down it. Try to find a crease in the rocks, where they have broken or started to erode. Telltale signs are grass, trees, or shrubs growing in the rocks (often the case in sandstone areas such as the Four Corners region). This can sometimes lead to a less-steep break in the rocks. Sometimes you can connect ledges or ramps, especially on Sierra Nevada granite.

In all cases, you never want to jump down anything! It can be easier to descend something than ascend. If you jump down, you might not be able to climb back up. You could end up cliffed out above and below, with nowhere to go. Always assume that if there is one drop-off in a canyon, there is likely to be more down below. Don't get fooled into thinking that the one you jumped down will be the only one.

The simplest solution to avoid getting cliffed out is to look at the map when you first get to a cliff area and see if there is an easy way around. Remember, without ropes and technical equipment, it doesn't take much to get cliffed out. We are only 5 to 6 feet tall with 3 to 4 feet of wingspan. If anything is over 10 feet tall, you are probably better off going around. Better safe than sorry.

Fording Dangerous Rivers

Fording a swift river is one of the most dangerous situations you can encounter on a hike. You can't always tell a river's depth, flow, or undertow by looking at its surface. Always approach creeks and rivers with respect and caution.

Depending on the size of the crossing, you can sometimes use downed trees to get across without even getting wet. That's always my go-to option if I can find it. My next favorite option is rock hopping across. Keep in mind that in some rivers, rocks may be glazed with moss, which can make them very slippery. Look for a greenish or brownish color on the upward end of the rock; this can warn you of perilous conditions. Sometimes when the temperature is below freezing, the top of rocks in a creek can be slick and icy from the splatter of the river water. In both of these cases, rock hopping is still possible, but trekking poles become very

A braided river in New Zealand with glacial origins. As you can see the water color can be milky making it difficult to tell how deep the river is and how the footing is. During times of heavy rain this river can fill the entire valley floor and be completely impassable. At lower flows you can choose areas to cross since the river braids divide the water flow into multiple channels and separate the volume.

important. So does scaling down the size of each maneuver between steps.

General river dynamics are also good to know. Here are a few helpful hints:

- Rivers are deeper under a steep bank and on the outside of a turn.

- They are shallower on the inside of a turn.

- Eddies behind rocks can help break the constant push of the river.

- Rivers typically meander slowly through meadows, and although the water may be deeper, the current is usually gentler, often making meadow areas safe places to cross.

Fast-moving water above the knee can knock someone over. Using trekking poles or a stick is very helpful both for balance and to test the depth of the water.

Glacial rivers are sometimes tough to cross because they are silty and you often can't see the bottom. However, they can also be braided and separated into various paths, helping diminish the intensity of the channel.

Do not do a tough ford barefoot! Unless the river is really gentle, wear shoes when fording a river. They help with traction and protect your feet in case there are jagged rocks in the water you can't see.

If the river looks too swift and is wide, look for a log across the river. If that isn't an option and you are on a long trip, scope out upstream to cross it. Sometimes that means miles upstream. But there's often less volume upstream, making the river easier to cross.

When crossing a river, I leave my sternum and hip belt straps buckled. Some people say you should unbuckle them so that you can get out of your pack quickly if you fall. I have done it both ways, and I find that I really don't like unexpected load shifts when I am in a precarious situation, which can happen when you're not strapped in. So I leave the straps buckled. If I do get submerged, I'm prepared to immediately unbuckle and ditch my pack. Also, I feel that people who say you should unbuckle straps are retelling tales from the old regime (you know, those old-schoolers with the big, heavy packs or external frame packs). With a trim, streamlined ultralight setup, your movements are not affected nearly as much. If you think someone is going to fall and you have an extra person in the group, you can have the extra person wait downstream. Make sure the catcher has something to help the person get to the shore, such as a solid tree branch, pole, or rope, just in case.

There are multiple ways to cross rivers. While there are other options, these have worked really well for me in some very tough situations.

How to Ford a Tough Crossing

1. Scout for a good place to cross the river before starting to cross. Rivers are dynamic and change often. Don't just assume that where the trail crosses the creek is the best and safest place to do so. Make sure exit and entry points are safe by looking for places where you will be able to ease into the water without losing your balance, stepping precariously, or stepping directly into fast-moving water. Also make sure you will be able to get out of the water without a struggle. Try to pick a spot where there are no visible rapids downstream, particularly with any downed trees strewn across—known as strainers. Getting swept into a strainer is one of the worst things that can happen. The branches dangling off the tree trunk down into the water can catch and keep you underwater and make it difficult or impossible to get out against the force of the rushing water.

2. Take off anything extra that is baggy, like rain pants, that can catch current. Tie your shoelaces and anything else you could trip over.

3. Sidestep across, without crossing your feet. Sidestepping helps prevent the push of the water from crossing up your legs and getting you off balance. Use your trekking poles for extra balance and also to test the depth of the water. Walk at a slight downstream angle while facing upstream. These tricks will make the river's current more manageable and make it easier to cross and less likely that you will lose your footing.

When Things Take a Turn for the Worst

If you get swept downstream, ditch your backpack immediately and swim for shore, whichever is closer or more manageable to reach. If you are caught in the current, float feet downstream and stomach up, using your feet and legs to cushion and bounce off rocks in your path. The only time you don't want to float in this fashion is when there is a strainer approaching. In this circumstance you want to go head first, stomach down, as though you are doing the butterfly stroke. As you near the strainer, try to lift yourself out of the water by putting your hands over the strainer, pushing yourself up, and kicking your feet. Do this to try to prevent yourself from going underneath it, where you might get pinned.

>>> TIP: Creeks, streams, and rivers rise and fall throughout the day. Often the most difficult crossings are raging from seasonal snowmelt or glacial runoff. If the body of water stems from snowmelt or a glacier, morning is the time of lowest flow and easiest time to ford. Sometimes the difference is substantial. I have seen creeks rise more than 6 feet between morning and afternoon—basically from fordable to deadly.

Hiking on Steep Snowfields

Snow creates unique hiking conditions. Snow conditions can change dramatically depending on recent weather, elevation, and time of year. You can bomb through a dusting of fresh, powdery snow or slog through miles of deep powder. Spring conditions are much different and vary throughout the day. Most hikers will typically encounter spring snow conditions and have to weigh the merits of carrying an ice axe and crampons. Trekking poles can be very handy for these situations.

Snowshoes generally aren't worth carrying for spring snow conditions. In spring the snow often has an icy crust in the morning. The crust can be treacherous on steep slopes, particularly when you can't kick steps into it. But it also makes travel fast and efficient. You can often disregard the actual location of the trail underneath the snow and take a shorter, more direct path.

Often there are cornices on saddles and passes. If you are trying to gain the pass or drop off the pass, it can be helpful to walk up a little to either side from the actual low point of the pass. Also, cornices can be overhanging and break off, so be careful when walking below them or getting too close to the edge. If necessary you can use the adze end of your ice axe to chop steps into the cornice.

Snow can melt out from underneath and be unpredictable. You might punch through into an air space and sink in deeply. Be careful when using snow bridges and when near rocks, especially in the afternoon when temperatures warm and the snow becomes softer.

Use the natural formations of the snow to help you create safe, flat platforms to step on. Trekking poles are also very helpful and provide increased balance and stability, as well as a makeshift ice axe if need be. *Photo by Shawn Forry*

On winter hikes and in spring snow conditions, plan where you camp and wake up early in the morning to take advantage of the best snow/hiking conditions. This will help you make good time. Traveling in the morning on firm snow will be faster, since you are on top of the snow rather than sinking into it like you will do in the afternoon, when you're postholing and expending a lot of energy in rotten snow. Also, try to walk in shady areas in the afternoon. The shaded snow isn't as rotten, and you won't posthole as much.

Although it is tempting to want to walk on rocks and get off the snow, keep the following in mind: Snow often melts from underneath, meaning you can sink deeper or even poke through an air pocket under the snow that's deeper than expected. Either take a big step on and off the rocks or give them a wide berth. Also watch out for thin snow bridges with water running underneath.

Take big steps when walking on and off snowfields. Snow is often slushy or punchy near the edges, and those are commonly the first places to soften with daytime warming. Areas that are firm and solid in the morning may require postholing in the afternoon.

If you're going to follow somebody's tracks through the snow, make sure they go where you want to go. For instance, Pinchot Pass on the PCT is a little confusing, and tracks can lead to the wrong pass. Check your maps often, and don't follow blindly.

>>> TIP: The last place snow refreezes overnight is under trees. If the temps are not dropping below freezing or are near freezing, open areas such as meadows and bowls can still refreeze due to radiational cooling. Tree cover prevents long-wave radiation from escaping, keeping such areas warmer. Snowpack is more solid and frozen in open areas and can still be punchy beneath trees. If you are below tree line, look for places where pine needles and plant debris have been deposited in the snow. These areas often stay icier and firmer throughout the day.

Spring snow conditions are what most PCT thru-hikers hit. The optimal plan for hiking through the Sierra Nevada in spring is to camp in a basin below the next pass. Wake up early and take an hour or two to get up to the headwall of the pass. If you're hiking northbound, the south side of the pass should be in morning sun and will get soft enough to get really good footing. By the time you get to the top of the pass, the north side should be softening up too. In the best snow conditions, you can glissade or "boot-ski" down the pass, ignoring the switchbacks of the trail, which are buried under feet of snow. This can save tons of time!

Even as you hike down the pass and into basins, snow conditions shouldn't be too soft or rotten. As you get lower into a basin in the Sierras, snow peters out. This is a good place to have lunch or take a break. If you're hitting another pass the next day, hike through the afternoon until you hit snow again. If you have the energy, posthole to get up a bit higher. If not, camp near the snow line, get up early the next morning, and cruise up to the next pass.

How to Ascend Steep Snowfields

1. When you're on snow and don't have crampons with you, route selection is very important. Snow can take the natural contours of the rocks underneath or completely cover them up. In some circumstances snow can fill in ledges and cliffs and make them scalable. Most important, when you look at the slope you will be ascending, consider two things: (1) If you have the option, ascend someplace with low exposure and low risk if you were to slip and slide down the slope. (2) Look all the way up to your goal. Does the pass have a cornice? Is it overhanging? Are there less-steep areas, rocks showing through, or ledges you can use to help you ascend more easily?

   Ascend so that you can attain your desired location to reach the pass/summit. Often cornices are like smiley faces. They are overhanging in the middle of the pass but can meet the ridgeline toward the corners. You can get on top of them without the hassle of chopping steps by simply ascending a bit higher and toward one of the corners. It is not always best to follow the route that the trail would have ascended up the headwall.

2. Since you don't have crampons with you, try to kick in steps on steeper terrain. Spring snow often naturally has little dimples and divots, like a golf ball. Use these natural platforms to your advantage, and kick steps into the snow in these natural depressions. Create a flat area by stamping your foot up and down and moving it from side to side or kicking your toe in sharply on tricky, firm slopes. This helps you get a good, flat position and creates something to anchor one foot on as you craft your next perch. If the snow is softening up, you can easily kick your toe in and ascend straight up the face or kick in the inside or outside of your foot to create a platform and ascend at an angle.

How to Traverse Steep Snowfields

1. Traversing a snowfield can be harder than ascending or descending. Eye the area where you want to go to. It may be where the snow ends, where the pitch mellows out, or where you can see the trail breaking out of the snow. It can be difficult to hold your line across the snow and move perfectly across.

2. Kick steps with the outsides and insides of your feet, making sure each foot is stable before planting to kick the next step. It can be helpful, especially on steep terrain, to traverse at a slightly ascending or descending angle.

1. Check your map, and look toward your descent. Pick out landmarks that will serve as guides and keep you on track. For example, go to the right of the first lake, to the left of the second lake, to the outlet of the third lake, on the right side of the creek, and/or below that ridgeline. Since descents can be very fast on snow and you won't be seeing signs of the trail, this will help you find the trail and continue making good time once the snow peters out.

2. If you have an ice axe, you can use the pick end to help control your speed. However, for a lot of hikes you won't be carrying an ice axe. In these circumstances it can be tricky to control your speed, especially if the snow is icy and firm. You need to try to traverse to an open area for the descent so that there's less consequence if you slip and speed down out of control. If you can, find an open bowl with a single fall line, no rocks, and a smooth, gentle run-out. Traverse to that area using the techniques described above.

3. If the snow is getting softer, you may be able to safely butt-slide down the slope and stay in control. If you are worried about staying in control, you can collapse your trekking pole and use it to help slow you down, as explained below. Another technique I often use when the conditions are softening is to boot-ski down, basically just skiing on the soles of my shoes. It can be really fun but hard to check your speed. You can also walk down fast using the "plunge step" method. This entails stepping down and digging your heels into the soft snow as you descend. You can move pretty fast this way, and gravity helps make it minimal effort. On the other hand, if the snow is still icy, you want to make sure

your descent stays completely under control. This can be a much slower process.

You can wait and take a break if you think the sun will hit the slope and warm up the snow. If there are multiple aspects around, you may be able to traverse a slope that has received more sun and will be softer, or you can just deal with it and pick your way down. Trekking poles can be very helpful. Use the dimples of the snow, and kick steps to create platforms for your feet. Do not try to go straight down; instead move back and forth across the slope, traversing and creating switchbacks.

>>> TIP: When hiking in snow, apply sunscreen early and often. People get roasted on the PCT in the spring. They get burnt from the reflection of sun off the snow. Be sure to get the bottom of your chin, your ears, under and in your nose, the back of your legs if you're wearing shorts, under your forearms—and any other place where sunlight can bounce off the snow and onto your skin. I have even heard of people burning the roof of their mouth from hiking with their mouth open. Also don't forget sunglasses. People go snow blind in the Sierras in spring!

When Things Take a Turn for the Worst

You tried traversing the steep snowfield but slipped and are heading down the slope, what should you do? You need to self-arrest, but you don't have an ice axe. Here's what to do:

- Get your body oriented so that your feet are downhill.

- If you are using trekking poles, flip a trekking pole around, as you would if you were walking with an ice axe, so that the tip is facing down. Hold the trekking pole near the tip or at the basket so you don't place too much torque on the pole and snap it. Get the pole so that it is at the base of your neck and your shoulder. Roll your body so it is face down, and put all your weight onto the pole tip, digging it firmly into the snow. At the same time, start kicking your toes into the snow repeatedly, one foot at a time. It can also help to crouch your body so that you can get more of your body weight onto your pole and your toes. This should stop you or at least decrease your speed so that it will get easier to stop as you continue these actions.

- If you aren't using trekking poles, do the same things as above, but instead of digging a trekking pole into the snow, you will be using your elbow. As you roll over onto your stomach, bend your arm and bring your hand up to your head. Dig your elbow into the snow and put all your weight onto your elbow. Follow the rest of the directions above.

>>> TIP: When hiking in the snow, always consider avalanche danger. Travel in low-angle areas, and try not to walk below steep slopes. Slopes of 30 degrees or greater are more prone to sliding. If hiking in a group through a dangerous spot, move one at a time from safe area to safe area, keeping your eyes on the person going through the treacherous spots.

Travel gently. Don't stand on the edge of cornices or try to break them off—unless you're intentionally trying to see if a slope will slide under the weight.

If you're traveling where avalanche danger is high, take all necessary precautions. Travel with a partner; carry a beacon, probe, and shovel; and know how to use them efficiently.

A sign of increasing instability during the typical freeze-thaw cycle of spring days is when you begin to posthole deeper than your boot top. This means the snowpack is becoming unconsolidated and not bonding or adhering well. In spring this is usually due to daytime warming and the amount of free water in the snowpack.

In spring, avalanche danger dramatically increases when there's fresh snow. These are usually wet slides, which are slower and start as a point release and spread from there. Rainfall can add weight to the snowpack, and snow is further destabilized from wider changes in temperature during the day and strong solar radiation.

Also, when the snow starts melting in spring, there's typically a lot of rockfall from the added water and freeze-thaw cycles. Stay clear of rock bands and below rock faces.

>>> TIP: If you've gotten in over your head in icy or snowy conditions, here's a way to make some cheap and ultralight crampons so that you can continue your hike. Head out to town and hit the hardware store. You can also send the necessary materials to yourself in a resupply box before the snowy section. For example, if you are hiking the PCT, you can include it in your bounce box or resupply box to Kennedy Meadows. You will need sheet-metal screws or $3/8$-inch screws. Half-inch screws are usually the best because they are long enough to stay secure without penetrating the insole. If you are using minimal or barefoot-style footwear, you will need to use shorter screws. Sheet metal screws are good because their heads have a lip that helps with traction. Insert eight to fifteen screws, depending on the pattern of the sole of your shoe, into the raised treads. A cordless drill with $1/4$-inch socket will do the job quickly, or you can screw them in by hand. Make sure to stop when the heads of the screws touch the outsole. Don't overtighten them. This is a cheap ($1 to $3) and easy crampon for your ultralight and emergency needs.

Other Situation and Skill How-tos

There are plenty of other situations that require quick thinking or mental toughness when you are out hiking that I have not covered in this book. I'll sum up some of them briefly here.

Mental Aspects of Hiking/Thru-Hiking

Hiking and thru-hiking can be mentally trying, and at times painful and grueling. There will be plenty of occasions that are not enjoyable, but the lows are balanced with the highs and bad times with the good. Often the miserable, tough, challenging days are the ones you reflect on and admire years later. Without overcoming these difficulties, the goals and accomplishments wouldn't be as rewarding.

Thru-hiking is an accumulation of mini-goals into a compilation. Plan for the entire trip, but focus on immediate targets so that the impending distances that need to be

Windy ridge walk in the Henry Mountains on the Hayduke Trail, Utah

covered don't overwhelm you. Focus primarily on the next resupply. Complete that section, then think about the next section. If you are getting burnt out, take some time off at a lake or on a mountaintop, or take a day off in town and relax. Don't look too far into the future; don't think about Maine when you are in Georgia. And remember these wise proverbs: "It's not about the miles, it's all about the smiles," and "It's about the journey, not the destination." Enjoy yourself; challenge yourself. When you stop having fun, it's time to look for something else to do.

Scrambling/Talus/Scree

When walking cross-country across talus and boulder fields, scope out your route and your goal on the opposite side. Look for flat areas and rocks to step on. Try not to step in between rocks with narrow gaps. It can help to stash or carry your poles in one hand so you can use your hands and arms as additional points of balance. Using your poles in boulder and talus fields greatly increases the chance of snapping your poles.

Crossing talus in the Canadian Rockies

Setting up a makeshift camp on the Packwood Glacier after the clouds rolled in. I couldn't see anything and couldn't tell where I needed to go to gain the knife-edge ridge on the PCT to the north. Better off playing it safe by stopping and waiting for it to clear. The next morning it was sunny and clear and I could safely proceed.

Whiteouts

If you are in a really bad whiteout, your best bet is often to set up camp and stay put until the weather improves. It is always better to stop early than to continue and put yourself into danger. It is easy to get off track when you can't see, especially if the ground is snow covered and you can't see or follow a trail. If you have a GPS unit with waypoints programmed in, it can be a great aid to allow you to "connect the dots" and keep moving, even though you can't see where you are headed. If you are trying to navigate with map and compass, it is very difficult when you are in a true whiteout. Before you get lost, set up camp and wait it out.

Quicksand

If you get stuck in quicksand, stop struggling. Take off your pack and try to toss it to the side of the quicksand. Spread out your arms and legs as much as possible, and

Pepper gets dirty in the Dirty Devil. Here Pepper is starting the horizontal move and spreading out his weight to help him get out of the quicksand. If you feel comfortable with an ultralight pack on, there is no need to remove it.

slowly fall forward to get as horizontal as possible. Now crawl or swim to firm ground.

If You Hear Banjos (Especially Dueling Banjos)...

Hike faster!!!!

The night before I drove to Georgia to start my first AT thru-hike, my mom laid down the law. She wouldn't let me leave the house until I had watched *Deliverance*. I am not sure what her intentions were, but to this day I still believe that on most hikes, other people are the most dangerous thing you can encounter. This may seem pessimistic, but I thoroughly believe that most animals are, or should be, scared of humans. On the other hand, there are a lot of strange people in this world and a lot of ill-advised hitchhiking rides to town for resupply. But if you insist, it is really important to try to give the car a once-over before you get in. Start a conversation asking if the driver is headed past your desired location. Evaluate his or her speech, overall mood, and any clues you see from looking into the car. Hitchhiking is the single most dangerous thing that a hiker does on a thru-hike. The percentages of incidents are low, but it is much more dangerous to be the hitchhiker getting into an unknown environment than being the driver. Countless times I have seen dozens of empty beer cans strewn all over the passenger side floor when offered a ride. I'll gladly wait for the next car to pull over instead of praying for my life heading down a windy mountain road.

In some foreign countries, Americans are associated with money. This can add another danger if you're hiking in these areas. Be smart, and follow standard travel precautions: Make photocopies of your passport, separate your money, do not take out large bills or large amounts of money to pay for things, be mindful of when you take your camera out, don't draw unnecessary attention to yourself, and don't leave your belongings unattended.

How to Build a Fire

Fires are the essence of camping and a key tool for survival, but under normal circumstances, I never build them. I can count on one hand all the times I have built a campfire. The majority of those times, the campfire was a miniscule twig smudge to create smoke to keep the mosquitoes at bay. However, one time I had to build a fire for a woefully unprepared Boy Scout outing. Two days of cold, steady rain and a scary amount of drenched gear and sleeping bags, moderately hypothermic 10-year-olds, and some panicking, in-over-their-head trip leaders made for an interesting find in the middle of nowhere.

It is crucial to pack your sleeping bag well so that it won't get wet. I pack my sleeping bag inside my backpack in a trash compactor bag, so I know I will have that warmth and security blanket no matter how bad the weather. My lighter is also deep inside my pack, in a zipper-lock baggie with my stove, and inside my pot, where it is very unlikely to get wet. If I am cold and wet, I know I can set up my shelter and get warm and dry in my sleeping bag. This prevents me from having to expend extra energy making a fire when it is raining and cold. However, it is essential to know how to start a fire in any situation, including with wet wood. Being comfortable making a fire can get you out of trouble and is one of your last lines of defense against the elements.

How to Build a Fire with Wet Wood

1. Accumulate some small pieces of wood, twigs, or dry leaves to get started. This may entail searching under trees, digging into lower layers of the duff, or using an inner layer of tree bark. Depending on your location, the optimal fuel sources for starting a fire will vary, but always try to find dry, downed wood.

2. Make a tepee with small sticks, and put some twigs and dry debris in the middle. Light the debris and small sticks using your lighter. If necessary, pour a little bit of your stove fuel onto the debris and sticks. You can also soak a stick or dip it into your fuel bottle before adding it to the fire. Don't go too heavy with the stove fuel; you don't want to use it all on the first try. You might need to add some more fuel if the first attempt doesn't work.

3. If the fire catches, let the sticks burn a bit and create some coals before you start adding more wood and slightly larger pieces. Build up the size of the additional wood so that you don't smother your fire. If need be, add a little more stove fuel to get things going. White gas is very volatile; it flares up and quickly dies down. Alcohol burns for a longer time but at a lower temperature. Both can be beneficial. Fire

travels upwards, so it can help to put the fuel below things that you are attempting to make catch.

4. If your fire still isn't lighting, remember to start small. Use small pieces of dry tinder. It can also be helpful to use your knife and strip off the wet outsides of the pieces of wood you are using. Try to get down to dry areas, and keep your fuel in a dry place. An abandoned bird's nest can make great tinder, as can dead lower limbs on evergreen trees. In Western forests, some coniferous trees accumulate large amounts of sap on the outside of the bark. Tree sap can also help you get your fire started. It catches easily and burns well.

When Things Take a Turn for the Worst

If the fire isn't starting no matter what you do and your sleeping bag is drenched, you need to set up your shelter and put on dry clothes or head for the car or for civilization, depending on the time of day. Know when to cut your trip short and head for the nearest trailhead. This may or may not be the same trailhead you entered from. Don't worry about that! You can get back to your car later, but for now you must think about your immediate well-being. Keep moving, and eat occasionally, even if you are not feeling hungry. Make sure to reference the map to keep on target as you head for civilization.

>>> TIP: If you are getting cold, you have a few options to stay warm: (1) Keep moving/hiking. (2) Do jumping jacks to get your blood moving. (3) Make a fire. (4) Eat something with a high calorie content; your body needs calories to stay warm. On cold, rainy days, it is tempting to push through without stopping. Your body needs to refuel. Keep snacks and a lunch handy so that you can take quick breaks or eat while you are walking.

>>> **TIP:** If you have some dry cotton, like a bandanna, you can make a char cloth to help you start the fire. Turn your stove on and place 2 × 2-inch squares of cotton in your pot; cover it. In a few minutes you should start to see a decent amount of smoke. When the smoke stops, shut off your stove and let it cool down. You should have charred squares of fabric that will easily catch a spark and burn slowly. When you blow on the char cloth, it should help your tinder burn. You can also use any petroleum-based product, such as Chapstick, DEET, or Vaseline, or your toilet paper stash to help get your fire started.

Lost in the Wilderness

There's lost . . . and then there's really LOST. The first lost is more of a temporary misplacement and easily takes care of itself. The second lost is the Oh $*#&! lost and is more serious. This is the type of lost you will need help to solve, and you may or may not be prepared for it. It's also possible that your maps no longer cover the area you have wandered into.

>>> **TIP:** Three blows on a whistle is a universal signal for help.

What to Do

1. Don't panic! Stay calm; stop and look at the map, using your last known point as a reference. People often consider just one possibility and attempt to make the terrain fit their assumption. Unfortunately, they're often in a different spot than they think they are.

    Consider all the possible places you could be on the map. Narrow it down to what fits, using landmarks to triangulate your location on the topo map. You can always retrace your steps to get back on track. If you can determine your location without a doubt, you may be able to figure out a different route to intersect your planned route.

If you're totally lost, STOP; remain calm, and evaluate the situation. Remember, "Undue haste makes waste." Try to remember any landmarks you passed or how long ago you made a turn that changed your course. Can you identify any obvious features (trails, roads, bodies of water, cliffs, changes in vegetation, etc.) that you recently passed? Think about how long you have until dark. If it's going to get dark before you can return to any known points, stay put and set up camp. It's better to set up at a place when you know you're lost than to push on in the dark and get even more lost.

If you're hiking with a group, talk things over and figure out a reasonable plan of action for determining your location and getting back on track. Don't act rashly! If you head out in one direction on a whim and have to backtrack, you end up wasting a lot of extra energy and time, and probably increase your worries.

>>> TIP: I can't emphasize this enough: Regularly check your position on the map; note where you think you are, and make a mental note of the time you are checking. You'll get to know your pace and where you should be at these intervals. Also check the time at known points, such as bridges, peaks, and other obvious features, as well as road, river, and trail crossings. That way, if you get lost, you will have an idea of how far from those features you've traveled and will have a better idea of where you are on the map.

2. If you need rescuing when you're lost, it can take hours or even days to be found. Help rescuers find

you by making a small smoke fire, or, if it's not too much effort, find an open area and lay rocks out in an X or a triangle formation. Also lay out some brightly colored clothes or your pack. Use something that will reflect sunlight onto planes flying overhead or anything else that might help. If you're lost at night, don't camp near running water. The water sounds will make it harder for you to hear voices or people nearby.

If you've called for a helicopter rescue or used a PLB (personal locator beacon), be ready to give details about your, or a patient's, condition. Details should include urgency, name, age, sex, and location. If calling, give them your best estimate of location, whether you intend to move, and, if so, where you intend to go. When a helicopter or plane flies over, stand toward it with your arms held in a V shape if you need help. If your arms are in a straight line at a diagonal, like a slash, it means "All OK." If you've managed to find your way before a rescue team arrives, change your PLB signal or call them back to call off the rescue effort. It costs a lot of money to organize and deploy rescue services—and you can be held liable for them.

>>> TIP: ALWAYS, always leave an itinerary and trip details with people you trust. Ideally, make sure they're in touch with one another as well. When on a long hike, I always give people my planned itinerary and resupply spots. I call or e-mail from each stop to let them know where I am and roughly when they should next hear from me. If they don't hear from me and it's more than a day late, they can initiate the search-and-rescue system, providing an idea of where I should be.

Without a compass or an altimeter watch, there are a few easy tricks to get your bearings.

Timekeeping and navigation. One of the most important tenets of good navigation is checking your location on the map at random intervals and matching your location with the time. That gives you an idea of both your pace and location. Then, if you get off course you can refer back to the last time you were still on course and have a better idea of where you are because you know where and when you were last on course. And you can make plans to either double back or adjust your route to get back on course.

Wear a watch, and know when sunset will occur. If your watch fails, knowing when sunset will occur can still help you figure out what time it is. Cover the sun with your thumb, palm facing you. Each finger above the horizon represents 10 to 15 minutes before sunset.

Navigation can be very challenging in areas without distinguishing characteristics and landmarks or when there is low visibility. Make sure to check your location and the time regularly so that you can narrow down your location if you get lost.

⟩⟩⟩ **TIP:** It is a common misconception that if you are lost you should try to follow a creek or river downstream to civilization. This is often not the best approach. In some areas rivers flow directly into the ocean and there are no civilizations along the route. In other places the river has carved a canyon with dangerous drop-offs and no possible exit. A map will dictate what you should do. But if you don't have a map, it is best to get a view from a high point and make your plans and travel the path accordingly. Your knowledge of settlements and the specific area you are in will also guide your egress route.

You can use the sun to tell direction using two methods. An analog watch face's hour hands can help you determine direction, as can a stick in the ground.

- In the northern hemisphere the sun is due south at noon (it's easier to tell before and after summer, when the sun travels lower in the sky).

   In the southern hemisphere the sun is due north at noon, again it's easier to tell when the sun is lower in the sky.

   When using an analog watch in the Northern Hemisphere to determine direction, point the hour hand in the direction of the sun, keeping the watch face flat. Halfway between the hour hand and the 12 is south. So if it's 5 p.m. in the Northern Hemisphere, south would be between 2 and 3. North is opposite that, and west and east are perpendicular. In the Southern Hemisphere, point the 12 on the watch face toward the sun. Halfway between the 12 and the hour hand is north.

- Alternatively, you can place a 3-foot-tall stick, your trekking pole, or something else upright in the ground. Mark the location at the end of the shadow.

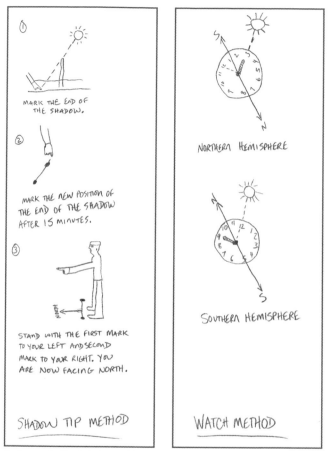

Daytime navigation techniques without a compass.

Wait about 15 to 20 minutes, and mark the tip of the shadow again. Draw a line connecting the two marks. This shows you an approximate east to west direction; you can calculate north and south by drawing a perpendicular line.

Nighttime Navigation: I don't recommend traveling at night when you are lost unless it is an emergency situation. The likelihood of getting increasingly lost or experiencing an additional injury increases while hiking at night, especially when hiking off-trail. Here are some nighttime navigation tricks.

- If the moon rises before the sun has set, the illuminated side will be the west side. If the moon rises after midnight, the illuminated side will be the east. This can provide you with a rough east–west orientation at night.

- In the Northern Hemisphere, you can tell north by finding the Big Dipper and Cassiopeia and locating Polaris (the North Star). These constellations and Polaris never set. The Big Dipper and Cassiopeia are always directly opposite each other and rotate counter clockwise around Polaris. The Big Dipper is made up of seven stars, with the two stars forming the outer lip of the dipper known as the "pointer stars" because they point to Polaris. Imagine a line from the outer bottom star to the outer top star of the bucket. Then extend the line about five times the distance between the pointer stars. The North Star will be along this line.

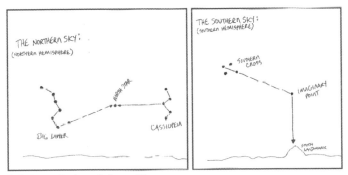

Nighttime navigation techniques without a compass.

Cassiopeia has five stars that form a W on its side. The North Star is straight out from Cassiopeia's center star.

After locating the North Star, you can locate true north (the direction to the North Pole) by drawing an imaginary line straight down to the horizon.

- In the Southern Hemisphere, look for the Southern Cross. It has five stars, and its four brightest stars form a cross that tilts to one side. The two stars that make up the long access are the pointer stars. To locate south, imagine a distance five times the distance between the pointer stars, and extend this distance from the lower pointer star. The point where the imaginary line ends is in the general direction of south. Look to the horizon, and locate a landmark below this point to act as a bearing.

>>> **TIP:** Try this trick if you can't find a map with distances between trail junctions or the key distances that you want to know. Hold a string to the map's scale, and mark the string to match miles, half miles, and so on. You can then use the string to provide fairly accurate distances on the map.

Signaling for Help with What You Have

Three of anything is considered the universal sign for help.

Here are the options to signal for help:

- Three consecutive blows on a whistle. Use two fingers if you aren't carrying a whistle.

- Three successive flashes from a headlamp or flash on your camera. It helps to be in an open area. Many headlamps now also have strobe features.

- Lay out bright clothes in an open area in a line or a triangle.

Shine the reflected sunlight through your fingers, then slowly alternate it back and forth so your fingers shade the reflection momentarily. Never hold the sunlight reflection directly into the cockpit for more than 3–5 seconds straight.

- Try using your cell phone to call or text; 911 calls will work on any network. If texting, text your location and condition to your entire contacts list. Save your battery by only turning on your cell phone for a few minutes each day.

- Make a fire in an open area to signal your location, or make three fires in the shape of a triangle. If it is the daytime and a fire will be hard to see, add wet leaves or green vegetation to create smoke.

- You can use your cell phone or GPS screen to reflect the sunlight between two fingers. Point the sun reflection at your target and move it back and forth between your fingers to signal.

- Pull a metallic-lined food wrapper tight and reflect the sun's light with it, signaling the same way as above.

If you move to a different location, make sure to leave signs indicating your direction of travel.

>>> TIP: When making a triangle using any of the above methods, remember that you are signaling to someone in the air. Try to contrast the color of the rocks against the ground. If you are on snow, get dark-colored tree branches or rocks. If you are in a meadow, get light-colored objects. Also make the triangle bigger than you might think you need. The sides should be at least 3 feet wide and 18 feet long.

Winter Survival

In winter, having a good shelter is the most important thing to help keep you alive. You have your shelter that you carried with you, but it can still be helpful to build a snow shelter. These shelters will help shield you from the wind and weather. In addition, the snow will help to insulate your shelter and keep the temperature inside from plummeting too much below freezing.

Wherever you're going, consider some of the additional backcountry dangers you may encounter in winter, primarily avalanches and whiteouts. If you're headed into avalanche country, beacons, probes, shovels, and the ability to use each of them are mandatory.

>>> TIP: Taking shorter breaks or eating while on the move will help prevent you from getting cold. When you do take a break, put on another layer before you get cold. Your body uses more energy to heat back up than it does to maintain the same temperature level.

Before you leave on a winter trip, however long, check the weather forecast. Check it again at resupplies so that you'll know what to expect and can plan and modify your itinerary accordingly.

It's important to stay dry in winter. Don't wear so many layers while traveling that you end up overheating or sweating. Balance your layers so you're neither too cold nor too hot. Wearing too many layers and getting hot and sweaty will only make you colder in the long run.

Things to Remember

Cold air sinks at night. To stay warmer, try not to camp in valley floors and low spots, where cold air accumulates.

When camping in winter, consider where the sun will come up in the morning and try to camp in a spot that will get first light. Try not to camp beneath a peak or in a spot that will be shadowed in the morning. It's really nice to get hit by early sun when it is cold out, and this will help get you motivated and moving in the morning.

>>> TIP: Caffeine restricts blood flow and cools extremities. If you get cold easily, you may want to steer clear of caffeine during winter camping trips.

Find shelter from the wind. Snowbanks, trees, windrows formed by wind on snow—all serve as wind protection. You can also make a wall out of the snow to the windward side of your tent. It helps break the wind and prevents your tent from getting buried if it is snowing or when snow is drifting in the wind. If you're using a tent, dig out a spot that's a few feet lower than the rest of the area. This way some of your tent is lower than the rest of the snow and more protected from the wind. Also, pack down the snow where you plan to set up your tent. It will make it more comfortable and less likely to melt.

Make sure you're safe from avalanches. Check trees for flagging (broken branches on their uphill side show evidence of past avalanches), prior avalanche debris in snow, and the terrain around you.

Winter Shelters with Nothing Extra to Carry

In winter you can use an all-season tent and often a three-season shelter or tarp, but you have some other options as well. You can make snow caves, igloos, trenches, or quinzhees. Each is a great option for winter camping; however, they can be time-consuming to make. If you're building it by yourself, allot about 2 to 3 hours. A trench is the fastest system to build.

An **igloo** is the most time-consuming and not the best method for lightweight hiking and backpacking; it can require a snow saw and takes a lot of work to pack the snow.

A **quinzhee,** or **quinzee,** is basically a snow cave, except you pile snow into a dome to make the cave because there isn't enough snow to dig a cave out. If you're making a quinzhee, make sure the snow settles enough to bond together. This can take a few hours, so you'll need to check it over time. Without proper snow consolidation, the roof may collapse.

〉〉〉 TIP: You can use an alcohol stove in winter. It just needs a little starter. Light a dry piece of paper or toilet paper, and hold the lit end to the alcohol. It will warm the fuel up and catch in a couple of seconds.

Snow caves require a lot of snow and a spot that's out of avalanche danger. Look for a snow bank or drift to build a snow cave in.

1. Start by digging a tunnel for the cave. The tunnel should be wider than your shoulders and should slope up toward the cave. That way cold air will settle outside the cave opening.

2. Hollow out a cavity in the snow for the cave. Make it tall enough to sit upright in and big enough for you and your companions to lie down in.

3. Pack the roof of the cave, and smooth the surface so that it doesn't drip on you or your gear.

4. If you have space in the cave, you can make benches out of the snow, keeping you off the ground and above some of the cold air.

5. Poke a trekking pole, ski pole, or probe through the ceiling of the cave for ventilation.

6. Cover the floor or the benches with waterproof material.

7. Put your backpack in the doorway to block cold air and keep the cave warmer.

Snow trenches are the easiest and fastest winter shelters to make, but they're not as comfortable or as warm as a snow cave. Also, they're not recommended if you're expecting a lot of snow, because they don't have strong roofs.

1. Dig a trench at least 3 feet deep, 6 feet long, and 3 to 4 feet wide for each person, with an entrance at one end.

2. Lay your poles, skis, or smooth tree branches across the width of the trench.

3. Spread your tarp, rainfly, or emergency blanket over the trench. Anchor the sides by covering the edges with snow, tree branches, or rocks.

>>> TIP: Keep your water bottle from freezing by only filling it three-quarters of the way and placing it upside down in your pack's side pocket. This prevents water from freezing in the bottle's mouth—unless it's really cold out. In extreme cold, keep your water bottle in an insulated pouch. You can also warm or boil your water before putting it in your bottle or the pouch. A thermos will also work but weighs more.

Drying and Preventing Gear from Freezing in Winter

Eventually your winter gear is likely to get wet, whether it's your shoes from hiking through snow all day or your gloves, socks or other layers of gear.

Since winter temperatures usually don't get above freezing, the only way to dry gloves and clothes is to wear them, hang them in your shelter at the top, or sleep with them in your sleeping bag.

>>> TIP: If new batteries aren't working in winter, it's most likely because they're cold. Warm them up in an inside pocket or close to your skin. You may also want to carry them in your pocket for a while when you know you are going to use your electronics.

When I have moist—not soaked—clothes at the end of the day, I prefer keeping them with me in my sleeping bag. I'll either wear them to bed underneath dry layers or put them in dead space within the sleeping bag.

Frozen footwear is painful to put on and wear. To keep your boots, shoes, or boot liners from freezing overnight, sleep with them in your sleeping bag's foot box or a dead space in your sleeping bag. If your boots are wet, put them in your inside-out pack liner or a stuff sack first—even if they're not going in your sleeping bag. Shake any dirt, mud, or excess snow off before putting them in your sleeping bag or in a stuff sack. Turn your pack liner inside out so that when you pack up the next day, you are still packing your gear into the dry side of the pack liner.

Ultralight Survival Skills
Fire (Bow-Drill Set)

Equipment needed: knife, wood from forest

Drill: best with cottonwood, birch, alder, sycamore, and willow

Fire board: best with cottonwood or dead willow

Tinder: inner bark of cottonwood or dry flammable material like shredded tree bark, bird's nest, or leaves

I have included a picture of a bow-drill set and the fire-plow method. If you need to choose between these, I recommend the bow-drill set. Both methods require energy, persistence, and practice; however, the bow adds mechanical advantage to the system and helps create additional friction.

It takes time to build a bow-drill set. I have built them on occasion for fun and to kill time. However, it only makes sense if your matches or lighter have stopped working and you are in an emergency situation where you are stationary and waiting for help. Otherwise, it is too time-consuming, and you'll likely be traveling to seek help or an exit out of

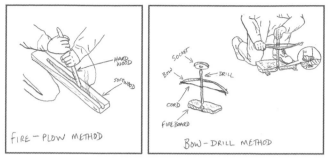

Fire plow and bow-drill set

the backcountry. Here are the basics of how to make this primitive fire starter.

Socket. Should be an easily gripped piece of hardwood, rock, or bone with a depression in one side. It is used to hold the drill in place and put downward pressure onto the drill.

Drill. A straight piece of seasoned hardwood about 2 centimeters in diameter and 25 centimeters long. The top end is pointed and the bottom end is blunt in order to focus the friction onto the fire board.

Fire board. Can vary in size based on available wood. Shoot for 2.5 centimeters thick and 10 centimeters wide. It could be a seasoned softwood or of the same material as the drill. Cut a depression about 2 centimeters from the edge on one of the long sides of the board. On the underside, opposite the depression, cut a V-shaped notch from the edge of the board to the depression. This will help to channel the punk (hot black powder) into a pile and create a coal. You can put a leaf or piece of paper underneath the notch to help transfer the coal to your tinder.

Bow. The bow should be made of a tough green stick. This will help it last longer and hold up to abuse. Look for one about 2.5 centimeters in diameter. It can be made of any resilient type of wood. The bowstring can be any type of cord. Tie the bowstring from one end of the bow to the other, without any slack.

To use the bow to make a fire,

1. Place some dry tinder, a leaf, or paper underneath the notch in the fireboard.

2. Place one foot on the fireboard. Loop the bowstring over the drill, and place the drill in the depression on the fireboard.

3. Place the socket in your other hand on top of the drill to hold it in position.

4. Press down on the drill and move the bow back and forth, spinning the drill.

5. Once you have the routine and a smooth motion, increase the downward pressure and the speed of the bow. It can help to place the wrist of the hand that is holding the socket directly against the shin of your leg that is stepping on the fireboard. This will add stability to the system as you increase the pace. The resulting increase in friction will cause punk to carry into the notch. Enough punk will result in a coal.

6. When you get a coal, or a glowing ember, collect the punk and place it in the "nest" of tinder. Blow in the tinder until it ignites.

Solar Still for Getting Water

Equipment needed: ground sheet or waterproof pack liner

Underground still. Dig a hole about 2 feet deep and line it with one or a half of your plastic pieces. Either pee into the plastic liner or add a bunch of green foliage into the hole. Put your pot in the center, lowest part of the hole, and on top of the liner. You can also throw some fresh foliage in there. Cover the hole with the other plastic piece, and place rocks around the border. Drop a small rock in the middle right over your pot so that the water/pee will condense on

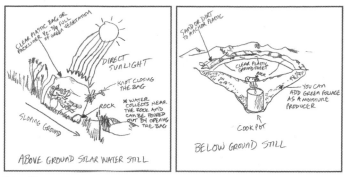

Solar still

the plastic and then drip down into the pot. This process can be used to get water and also to treat it.

Aboveground solar still. Put green foliage into your pack liner. Weigh one corner down with a rock, and tie the mouth of the bag closed above that. Place the bag in direct sunlight. Remove the water by untying the mouth of the bag and pouring out the water. Then reseal the bag to collect more.

Cloth Technique for Getting Water
Equipment needed: bandanna or base layer

You can collect condensation, dew, or steam from boiling water with your bandanna or base layer. Then you can wring out the bandanna to provide water.

Emergency Sleeping Bag or Sleeping Pad
Equipment needed: ground sheet or waterproof pack liner

You can crawl into your pack or pack liner and fill it with pine needles, leaves, grass, dry moss, and duff to create insulation. The same for a sleeping pad, but you sleep on top of it.

Emergency Vapor Barrier Liner

Equipment needed: Ground sheet or waterproof pack liner

Sleep with your feet inside your trash compactor bag on the inside of your sleeping bag in order to bump your sleeping bag up a notch. Your feet are often the first thing to get cold, so this will help keep you warm on a night colder than you were prepared for.

Sunglasses

Equipment needed: Cord and possibly duct tape

You can use webbing or tree bark, such as birch bark, or make a solid sheet from layering duct tape. Cut it to fit your face, and cut a small slit for each eye. Poke a hole to punch the cord through, and tie an overhand knot onto each end. This will prevent excessive amounts of light from entering your eyes and help prevent snow-blindness. You can also put some ash streaks underneath your eyes, similar to baseball players wearing eye black. This helps to reduce glare.

Time to Spare

You are out in the backcountry to relax, unwind, and enjoy yourself. It's inevitable that there will be some downtime, even if you are thru-hiking. Here are some things to do:

My go-to is to bring crossword puzzles and sudokus with me. I cut them out from the newspaper for a couple of months ahead of time and then pack some and include some in my bounce box so that I can pick up more along the way. They're an ultralight time sink and brain stimulant. While hiking, I often find myself pondering clues that stumped me the previous night.

If you are with kids, they always love skipping/skimming flat rocks in water and seeing how many times they skip.

When with a group of friends, it can be fun to talk with one other person and come up with four random words. You tell someone else the words, and he or she must use those

Time to spare in the backcountry can lead you to create some fun games and memorable times. You never know what you will find for entertainment on the side of the road or in a backcountry hut.

words in the remainder of the day or a set amount of time. It is kind of like a reverse mad lib. The rest of the group has no clue that they must use those words, so they'll think their friend is being really kooky. It can be pretty funny.

One of my favorites for group camping is to take a gallon-size zipper-lock baggie and set it on the ground, with the open mouth of the bag as its base. Make a line a foot or two back. Players must stand on one foot, without touching any other part of their body to the ground, and pick up the bottom of the baggie using their mouth. After each round, cut 1 inch off the mouth end of the baggie. If your hands or other foot touches the ground, you are out!

To play backcountry golf, use a pinecone or ball, grab a stick or trekking pole, and make up a target or hole. It's like golf and disc golf, but you have to play through everything—poison oak, bushes, boulders, or any other obstacle that stands in your path.

Sometimes I try to find some good pieces of wood and whittle. Sometimes I make spoons; other times I try to make little Buddhas. Most often I make bow-drill sets and experiment with different types of wood. This can be a great way to relax and pass the time.

Quick Gear Checklist

Here's a generic checklist to check off if you're scrambling to pack up and run out of the house. Tailor it to the season and place you are headed. Also consider making copies of the list and then tailoring it to your needs depending on the season.

Item	Weight	✓
Backpack		
Pack liner		
Sleep system		
Sleeping bag		
Sleeping pad		
Shelter and tent stakes		
Ground cloth		
Clothes		
Socks (__ pairs)		
Rain jacket		
Wind jacket		
Insulating jacket (down or synthetic)		
Rain pants		
Wind pants		
Beanie		
Gloves		
Food and water		
Stuff sack (for food bag)		
Cookware (pot, stove, windscreen, spork, fuel, lighter)		
Water treatment		
Water bottle		
Water bladder		

Item	Weight	✓
Accessories and necessities		
Ditties, book, maps, trail info, knife, pen, paper, extra batteries, and SD card for camera		
Toiletries (toothbrush, small toothpaste, floss, contact lenses and solution, glasses, sunglasses, toilet paper, etc.)		
Town necessities (credit card, ID, keys, and cash)		
Camera		
GPS unit		
PLB/Satellite phone		
Duct tape rolled onto your trekking pole or fuel bottle		
Clothes worn		
Watch		
Boxers		
Socks		
Shirt		
Shorts		
Hat or visor		
Trekking poles		
Shoes		

Index

About Trauma

Justin Lichter, aka Trauma, grew up in Briarcliff, New York, about an hour north of New York City. After college he quickly shunned the traditional career path and lived in southern Vermont; Dillon, Colorado; and Truckee, California, as he followed snow and his passion for skiing. When not hiking, Justin works as a ski patroller. Recreationally he enjoys backcountry skiing, Nordic skiing, snowshoeing, mountain biking, surfing, and anything else active and outdoors.

Since 2002 Justin has hiked more than 35,000 miles, equal to nearly one and a half times around the earth. His passion started in 2002 when he took an outdoor education class through the University of California at Santa Cruz. In this class they mostly traveled cross-country through the canyon country of southern Utah. On this trip, Justin started developing the idea of setting off on the Appalachian Trail. The following year, 2003, he hiked from Georgia to Cap Gaspe, Quebec, following the Appalachian and International Appalachian Trails.

The next year he undertook the Pacific Crest Trail from Mexico to Canada and then continued on the Pacific Northwest Trail to the Washington coast. Justin finished his first Triple Crown of long-distance hiking in 2005 upon completing the Continental Divide Trail from Mexico to Canada. He didn't stop there—he continued to hike north from the Canadian border on the Great Divide Trail to Kakwa Lake, British Columbia. Upon completing the Triple Crown, Justin looked for an opportunity to challenge himself and push the limits of human endurance—and find a good excuse to be outside and hike for a year straight. From November 1, 2005, to October 23, 2006, he completed the Eastern Continental Trail (Cap Gaspe, Quebec, to Key West, Florida, incorporating the AT), the Pacific Crest Trail, and the Continental Divide Trail in under a year, a total of more than 10,000 miles in 356 days.

The following year, Justin and frequent hiking partner Pepper developed a precursor to the Te Araroa Trail in New Zealand and traversed the Southern Alps and the South Island of New Zealand from south to north.

The list continues. In 2007 he swam unsupported around Lake Tahoe without a wetsuit and developed and hiked a route from Durango, Colorado, to Las Vegas, Nevada. In 2008 Justin hiked the Hayduke Trail through Utah and Arizona, traversed Iceland on foot, and hiked through Norway and Sweden. The next summer Justin ambitiously hiked 1,800 miles, solo and unsupported, through Africa, including crossing through Ethiopia and Kenya, before ending his trip after being stalked by lions. In 2011 Justin completed a traverse of the Himalaya Mountain Range from the eastern Nepal border to the India-Pakistan border.

Justin continues to work as a ski patroller in winter and is constantly dreaming up new adventures.